AN A-Z OF LIFE COACHING
TOOLS, TIPS AND TECHNIQUES

By

ELLIE BULL

Ellie Bull © Copyright 2020

All rights reserved.

No part of this publication may be reproduced, distributed or transmitted in any form or by any means, including photocopying, recording or other electronic or mechanical methods, without the prior written permission of the publisher, except in the case of brief quotations, reviews and other noncommercial uses permitted by copyright law.

"Coaching is unlocking a person's potential to maximise their own performance. It is helping them to learn rather than teaching them"

- Sir John Whitmore

Contents

Foreword vii

What coaching is (and what it isn't) 1

- A is for Analysing your Client 9
- B is for Beliefs 23
- C is for Circle of Influence 28
- D is for Delving Deeper 31
- E is for Exploring Change 33
- F is for the FEAR Model 38
- G is for the GROW Model 42
- H is for Homework 47
- I is for Initial Call (or Discovery Call) 49
- J is for Journaling 53
- K is for Key Coaching Skills 56

- L is for Language 66
- M is for MBTI 77
- N is for NLP 100
- O is for OSKAR Model 110
- P is for Progress Reviews 113
- Q is for Questionnaires 116
- R is for Reframing Techniques 119
- S is for Setting Goals 124
- T is for Timeline Technique 131
- U is for Understanding Goals 137
- V is for Values 140
- W is for Wheel of Life 144
- X is for (e)Xtra Exercises 149
- Y is for You (as the coach) 154
- Z is for Generation Z 161

Afterword 169
Endnotes 171

Foreword

Greetings, established and aspiring coaches. I hope this book finds you well.

Whilst there is much more to the art of coaching than just the use of various models and frameworks, I have found that they can be especially useful in the early days of one's coaching career in order to provide structure and form.

On that basis, I have designed this handbook as a collection of easily digestible, accessible coaching tools, techniques and models for you to use in your coaching work. You will find that they are organized in an A-Z style of format to enable you to flick between chapters and refer back to specific topics with ease.

There is a vast amount that can be learned on the subject of coaching and it is impossible to cover everything in one book, so this is by no means an exhaustive list, but hopefully you will find the assortment provided as a good starter for ten.

Being able to help clients improve their lives through the medium of coaching can be an incredibly rewarding experience. Luckily for us coaches, people all around the world are waking up to its value, and this has been reflected in how much the industry has grown over the last few years. As of 2019, the coaching industry had an estimated value of £11 billion worldwide and the expectation is that this figure will continue to grow.

Coaching is a highly beneficial discipline that can enrich the lives of many if done well. I hope that this book arms you with a sturdy metaphorical toolkit for you to use in your future coaching endeavours.

To support you further, the full range of coaching exercises covered in this book are available for download at www.elliebull.com/coachingworksheets

What coaching is
(and what it isn't)

First, let us begin by clarifying what coaching is and what it is not.

There is no single agreed definition of coaching, which is unsurprising, given the rich and varied nature of the field.

Here are three of the definitions that I think explain coaching best.

Coaching is...

> 1. ...*An ongoing partnership that helps clients produce fulfilling results in their personal and professional lives. Through the process of coaching, clients deepen their learning, improve their performance and enhance their quality of life.*[1]
>
> - International Coaching Federation

2. *...Unlocking a person's potential to maximise their own performance. It is helping them to learn rather than teaching them... we are more like an acorn which contains within it all the potential to be a magnificent oak tree. We need nourishment, encouragement and the light to reach toward, but the oak-treeness is already within.[2]*

– John Whitmore

3. *...A collaborative solution-focused, results-orientated and systematic process in which the coach facilitates the enhancement of work performance, life experience, self-directed learning and personal growth of the coachee.[3]*

- Association of Coaching, UK

You can also describe coaching as a form of development in which a coach supports a client to raise their own awareness, take responsibility, think through options and ultimately decide upon their own course of action.

There is a big difference between teaching somebody something and helping them to learn. In coaching, it is all about helping the individual to improve their own performance. Good coaches believe that the individual always has the answer to their own problems but understands that they may need help to find the answer.

Under the broad umbrella of 'coaching' you'll find many different types and styles, some of which include:

- Career Coaching
- Executive Coaching
- Relationship Coaching
- Confidence Coaching
- Nutrition Coaching
- Mindset Coaching
- Retirement Coaching

Regardless of what your coaching niche may be, I would argue that all types of coaching can benefit from the use of certain models and techniques. Of course, some may be more relevant than others, depending on the area of coaching in which you specialise.

Coaching can often get grouped together with other forms of 'helping work', so to avoid any confusion, let us quicky look at what is coaching *is not?*

IT'S NOT COUNSELLING

Counselling is more likely to involve understanding and working with **past** experiences. A client's motive for entering counseling is often to get away from pain or discomfort, rather than moving towards desired goals. Coaching is not remedial, it is generative.

IT'S NOT CONSULTING

Coaching *does not* rely on a one-way flow of telling and instructing. A consultant provides expertise and solves business problems, or develops a business as a whole. A consultant deals with the overall organisation or specific parts of it and not individuals within it.

IT'S NOT TEACHING

Teaching passes knowledge from teacher to student. The teacher knows something the student does not. The opposite is true in coaching: the client is the expert and the client has the answers, not the coach.

IT'S NOT MENTORING

Mentoring is usually when a senior colleague, or an individual seen as more knowledgeable and worldly-wise, gives advice and provides a role model. Mentoring involves wide ranging discussions that may not be limited to the work context. Similarly to coaching, mentoring tends to be focused on the achievements of the present and future as opposed to the past, but unlike coaching the mentor is likely to have a significant professional experience in their client's field of work, whereas a coach does not need to have experience in the same field as their client.

One of the main differences is that coaching *is not* about providing advice. When I first started practicing coaching, one of the first things I struggled with was resisting the urge to give my client advice. I'd be listening to someone talk about an issue they were having, and I would have to fight the urge to jump in and make some form of practical suggestion as to what might help them solve it. These urges are normal and they come from a good place. After all, individuals who are drawn to the discipline of coaching tend to be the kind of folk who like to help others, and that's an admirable trait. However, it is vitally important that we understand why giving out advice to clients is, for the most part, actually doing them a disservice.

The whole premise of coaching is based on the belief that people *already know* the answers to even their most difficult and complicated challenges, and that they just need the time, space and some gentle guidance in order for them to find their way to their own realisations and breakthroughs.

We believe, as coaches, that if we jump in and interrupt that process, we can be inhibiting our client's own resourcefulness and denying them of new connections in their brain. What I mean by this is demonstrated in the 2009 research on 'financial advice and decision-making' by Jan B Englemann, et al[4]. Their findings illustrate that the brain "offloads" when it is receiving advice. This means that it goes into a type of 'neutral mode' and the advice does not embed in the neocortex whilst it is being given. Ownership of the advice may happen later on, but it also may not happen at all. This research means that as coaches we must instead look to engage all areas of our client's brain during the session by asking carefully positioned questions that require them to search inside themselves for the answers.

By allowing our clients to come up with their *own* solutions to their challenges, we, as coaches, are empowering them and empowerment leads to increased levels of self-belief and confidence, which can only be a good thing.

Before we move on, let us end this chapter by looking at what are known as the '5 Golden Rules of Effective Coaching':

1. **Be present in the room**

    This sounds obvious, but the quality of attention given by a coach to a coachee makes all the difference and helps to create a trusting relationship. It's important to ensure that mobile phones are switched off and that there are no other external distractions during the coaching session. Even if you are conducting coaching sessions remotely, which is increasingly common, the same premise applies.

2. **Ask questions**

    We'll be covering a lot of different coaching questions in this book, and that's because it's such a big part of successful coaching. An interaction in which the coach is doing most of the talking is more likely to fall into the category of mentoring or consulting than it is coaching. With coaching, we want the client to do most of the talking as they explore the questions that we have asked them.

3. **Seek to understand, not judge**

    It is important to seek to understand the other person, rather than judge them. Behaviour that implies a judgement from the coach is not usually effective and can damage rapport. The deeper you understand a person the more likely you are to help them change their behaviour.

4. **Listen**

   Again, this should go without saying, but there is no point asking questions if you don't listen to the answers. The quality of listening is absolutely key in coaching. You need to be able to listen to the whole person and not just the surface level noise.

5. **Focus on action**

   Effective coaching is about raising the coachee's awareness of themselves and their behaviour and enabling them to take responsibility for change.

Now that we are clear in our heads what coaching is and isn't, we can begin to look at some of the useful models that are out there, with the aim of expanding our coaching repertoire.

A is for Analysing your Client

If we are going to create change for somebody, shift their perspective, break down their barriers and build a connection, we must first understand the person in front of us and how to communicate effectively with them. Only through effective communication will we be able to help them to achieve results.

In terms of how we can do that, we must seek to analyse various elements of our client's behaviour early on, in order for us to know how to adapt our coaching style accordingly.

In this chapter, we are going to talk about analysing:

- Representational Systems
- Learning Styles
- Behaviour Patterns

ANALYSING YOUR CLIENT'S REPRESENTATIONAL SYSTEM

How we process information is related to what is known as our 'Representational Systems' (or rep systems for short). This is an NLP term, which we will be looking more at later on in this book.

The three main rep systems are known as: 'visual', 'auditory' and 'kinaesthetic'. All of us use all three systems in our daily lives, but everyone tends to have one *lead* rep system (which is the one we use the most).

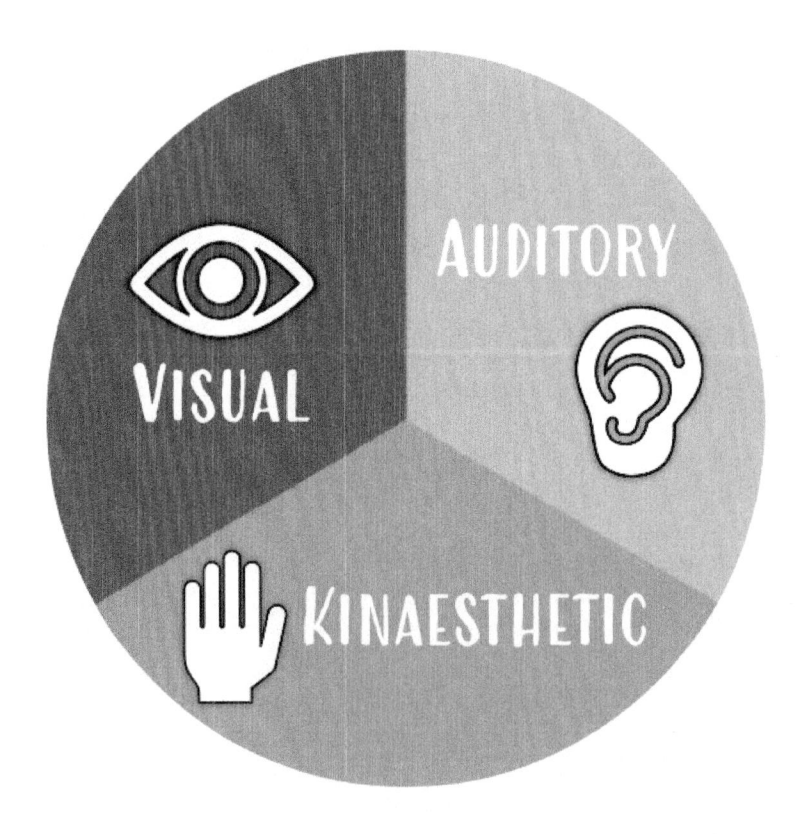

Think about when you walk into a room full of people – what is the first thing you become aware of?

- **Visual**: What you see. Is your attention first drawn to the people, the colours, the movements, individual faces?
- **Auditory**: What you hear. Are you first drawn to the sounds or conversation, the high and low voices, laughs, tinkle of glasses or cutlery?
- **Kinaesthetic**: What you feel – physically and emotionally. Do you first pay attention to the temperature of the room, the feeling of the flooring and furniture – or are you attending to feelings such as the mood in the room or your own feelings?

The benefit of working out which rep system your client uses predominantly, is that you can start to *speak their language*. They will find information much easier to process if it's presented to them in language which reflects their preferred rep system. I'll explain how to do this later on.

First, let's look at how we work out which rep system our client leads with. There tend to be some giveaways in our language and our nonverbal cues.

Language:

- **Visual** sensory language involves thinking in pictures and images. Clients who are visual usually find diagrams and mind map helpful in gaining an understanding of their issues, and because they frequently work well with metaphors, they often use colourful language. A client might say things like this:

"I *see* what you're saying"

"I'm *picturing* it"

- **Auditory** sensory language is all about the importance your client places on sound. Their hearing is finely tuned, and they are often musical or love music. They learn best through hearing themselves think aloud, and through discussions, audio books and talks. Clients may make comments like:

"I like the *sound* of doing that tomorrow"

"I *hear* what you are saying"

- **Kinaesthetic** sensory language is a preference for body and feelings-based expression, where clients use metaphorical, physical or feeling words. They learn best through experimentation and experience. Clients may express themselves like this:

"My *gut reaction* is that it's a good idea"

"It *feels* like a good idea"

Nonverbal cues:

- **Visual** individuals will tend to move their hands at shoulder or head level, sit upright and give importance to their visual appearance. They will also have a tendency to move their eyes upwards (straight up or up to the left/right) when recalling an event.

- **Auditory** individuals tend to breath from the middle of their chest, get easily distracted by noise, and gesture on chest level. Their eye movements will tend to be from side to side (towards their ears) when recalling an event.

- **Kinaesthetic** individuals will tend to have low breathing from the belly, stand quite close to whoever they are talking to, and have low and smooth gestures. Their eyes may look downwards towards their body when recalling an event.

If you are still struggling to tell, here is a very short quiz[5] that you can have your client do which should give you an indication. Mostly (A) answers = Kinaesthetic, mostly (B) answers = Visual, and mostly (C) answers = Auditory.

1. If you were buying a new household appliance, you would:
    A. Fiddle with the knobs and test it out
    B. Read about the various models
    C. Talk about it with others

2. Recalling _____ is usually easiest for me:
    A. Experiences
    B. Faces
    C. Names

3. When having an issue with an item you bought, you more often:
   A. Take the item back
   B. Write a letter to the company
   C. Call and complain

4. When you are showing someone else how to do a new task, you typically:
   A. Show them how, and then let them give it a go
   B. Write out step by step directions
   C. Give them a verbal walk-through

5. When cooking a new type of meal, I prefer:
   A. To just start cooking, and feel my way through it
   B. To follow a recipe
   C. To call someone else to ask how it is prepared

6. My very first memory is about:
   A. Something I did
   B. Something I saw
   C. Hearing a familiar voice

7. When meeting someone new, my first impression is of:
   A. Their posture or pose
   B. How they look
   C. What they say

8. When speaking, I more typically say:
   A. I understand how you feel
   B. I see what you're saying
   C. I hear you

9. When you have spare time, which is your stronger preference:
   A. Gardening or participating in a sport
   B. Going out and seeing new things
   C. Talking with others or listening to music

10. If you were to install a new doorknob for the first time, you would:
   A. Figure it out as you go
   B. Read the directions
   C. Ask someone else how to do it

So why does knowing this information help us in our coaching? Well, an awareness of your client's representational system preference will help you to understand how your client filters and perceives the world. It will also reveal how they best receive information, how they learn, and what's the best way to deliver feedback effectively. You will become better attuned with them and you may even be able to adapt your style to match your client's way of working, creating a powerful kind of emotional mirroring.

For example, you can adapt your own language to suit theirs:

"How would things look for you if you were to do X",

"Where do you see yourself in a year's time?"

or

"I hear what you're saying"

"How does that <u>sound</u> to you?"

or

"How would you <u>feel</u> if that were to happen?"

"How would you like to <u>feel</u> moving forward?"

ANALYSING YOUR CLIENT'S LEARNING STYLE

Analysing your client's learning style might seem a little strange on the surface, however, this information can provide you with the necessary insights you need to help guide your client down the right path more effectively.

As a coach, you will be setting your client homework, exercises, tasks and activities that you would like them to complete over a specific time period. Thoroughly understanding your client's learning preferences will allow you to set these tasks in optimal ways that will keep your client focused and motivated

When it comes to learning styles, your client is likely to have a preference for one of four[6]:

THE ACTIVIST

The first learning style is the Activist. An Activist prefers time-framed activities; they seek involvement in a task and they learn best while taking risks. As such, it's important to set them tasks that have clear dates and deadlines. It's also important to challenge them to step out of their comfort zone and get involved in a task straight away. Make sure you set them various activities that will put them into learning situations, while also ensuring that there's enough variety in these activities to keep their interests alive.

If your client answers 'yes' to these questions it may indicate that your client has an Activist learning style.

- *Do deadlines help motivate you?*
- *Do you have a tendency to take risks?*
- *Do you consider yourself to be an optimistic person?*
- *Do you feel comfortable making mistakes?*
- *Do you get bored easily doing the same things over again?*

Keep in mind while setting tasks for an Activist that they have a tendency to take quick action without weighing up other possibilities. They also tend to want to do too much by themselves. Moreover, they sometimes take unnecessary risks and can get bored when it comes to implementing things long-term. However, they are often very open-minded, optimistic, enthusiastic, willing to have a go, and enjoy new experiences.

THE REFLECTOR

The second learning style is the Reflector. A Reflector dislikes deadlines. Instead, they prefer to learn by watching, listening and by journaling their thoughts and experiences on paper. Above all else they prefer thinking tasks that challenge them intellectually. As such it's important to set them activities that allow them time to think and reflect upon things before taking action.

If your client answers 'yes' to these questions it may indicate that your client has a Reflector learning style.

- *Do you prefer to think and reflect before you act?*
- *Do you tend to procrastinate and make decisions slowly?*
- *Do you tend to hold yourself back from participating in activities?*
- *Do you enjoy observing things from afar?*
- *Do you enjoy intellectual challenges?*
- *Do you tend to feel uncomfortable during pressure situations?*

Keep in mind while setting tasks for a Reflector that they have a tendency to procrastinate. They will also hold themselves back from direct participation in an activity and prefer to let other people take the spotlight. Reflectors are also very passive and slow to make up their minds about things. As such, they tend not to take risks. However, they are often very careful, thorough, methodical, thoughtful, and fully assimilate information without jumping to quick conclusions.

THE THEORIST

The third learning style is the Theorist. A Theorist enjoys connecting and making associations between things. They love gathering new information, insights, and perspectives then using this new found knowledge to improve their life. They are often very logical, objective, systematic and analytical. In some respects, they are very much perfectionists by nature and will, therefore, do everything within their power to ensure that they avoid making mistakes. As a result, they learn best using a rational approach. It's therefore important to set them tasks that involve a lot of research so that they can make sense of their world and circumstances before taking positive action.

If your client answers 'yes' to these questions it may indicate that your client has a Theorist learning style.

- *Would you call yourself a rational thinker?*
- *Would you consider yourself to be a disciplined person?*
- *Do you enjoy making connections and associations between things?*
- *Do you often conduct research before you take action on a problem?*
- *Do you see yourself as a perfectionist?*
- *Do you tend to feel uncomfortable when faced with uncertainty?*

Keep in mind while setting tasks for a Theorist that they are limited in their creative capacity. They also have a low tolerance for uncertainty, disorder, and ambiguity. Above all else, if something doesn't make rational sense, then they will resist the idea. As such all the tasks and activities you set for them must be of a rational and measurable nature. However, a Theorist is very disciplined once they are committed to something, but they will tend to question the rational purpose of any task you set.

THE PRAGMATIST

The fourth learning style is the Pragmatist. A Pragmatist enjoys solving problems and laying down their own path towards their goal and objective. They have a very practical approach to life and therefore learn best via real-life experiences. As such, it's important to set them tasks that are practical and challenge their capacity to solve real-world problems. In fact, provide them space and time to experiment and make mistakes. Even better, allow them to set their own tasks and plans of action for solving problems. That is after all how they work best.

If your client answers 'yes' to these questions it may indicate that your client has a Pragmatist learning style.

- *Do you prefer to set your own plans?*
- *Would you call yourself a practical and realistic thinker?*
- *Do you get impatient with theories that don't have any practical application?*
- *Do you have a task-oriented nature?*
- *Do you enjoy experimenting and learning from experience?*
- *Do you prefer to solve your own problems?*

Keep in mind while setting tasks for a Pragmatist that they have a tendency to reject anything without obvious application. They also show disinterest in theories and can become rather impatient very quickly. Furthermore, they are often more task-oriented rather than people-oriented. However, they are often keen to test things out in practice and they have a very business-oriented approach to their problems. In other words, a Pragmatist always likes to get to the point straight away.

As you can probably tell, each learning style has very different preferences for learning. These preferences help keep people motivated and focused on the right things while undertaking tasks and activities.

As coaches, it is beneficial for us to know this information about our client so that we can adapt our coaching approach accordingly.

ANALYSING YOUR CLIENT'S BEHAVIOUR PATTERNS

It is often our behaviour patterns that prevent us from achieving our desired outcomes, so it is important to pinpoint early on what behaviours might be hindering your client from moving forward.

Begin by asking your client:

- *Are you getting the results you desire to have in your life?*
- *Why do you think you are not getting these results?*
- *What behaviours, rituals, and/or habits might be letting you down?*
- *How are your behaviours preventing you from getting what you want?*
- *Where are your present behaviours taking you?*

These questions will at the very least provide your client with a wake-up call. No longer will they be ignorant of the behaviours they consistently indulge in throughout the day. They should now begin to question their daily choices, decisions and actions moving forward.

Your main objective here is to use this process to help unlock patterns that are holding your client back. However, these patterns might not be straightforward. There might, in fact, be some underlying causes of your client's behaviour. These causes can come in the form of limiting beliefs, unhelpful thoughts, and a poor self-concept, which can ultimately manifest in a fear of some kind. You might, therefore, need to explore each of these areas in a little more detail.

Remember, the more you know about your client's preferences and behaviours, the better equipped you are to build a strong working relationship with them and help them to achieve their goals.

B is for Beliefs

A belief can be defined as: *"An acceptance that something exists or is true, especially one without proof".*[7]

Everyone has beliefs, and these will be a mixture of what we, in the coaching world, call: 'Empowering Beliefs' and 'Limiting Beliefs'.

These terms basically mean beliefs that serve and benefit us, and beliefs that hold us back in life.

You will find that clients have limiting beliefs about all sorts of things. Their abilities or potential, their identity as a whole, their behavior and even about other people.

These limiting beliefs often lead to fear, self-sabotage, negative thinking, procrastination and all manner of other unhelpful outcomes.

As coaches, it is our job to try and get to the bottom of our client's beliefs, especially their limiting beliefs. Because thankfully, beliefs, just like opinions, can ultimately be changed.

Limiting beliefs are the number one reason why your client will be struggling to see results in their life, so if we can break these limiting beliefs down, the chances are we can greatly improve the lives of our clients.

Here is a process that you can follow to try and combat your client's limiting belief:

1. Listen out for the limiting belief
2. Highlight it to the client
3. Challenge it through your questioning
4. Encourage them to take action towards their goal in order to start a positive belief cycle

LISTEN OUT FOR THE LIMITING BELIEF

You should be able to pick up on cues in the language they use to identify the limiting belief. Statements such as:

"I'm not smart enough/fit enough/good enough"

"I couldn't do X because of Y"

"I don't believe I can/will..."

"I will probably fail"

The chances are that your client will have more than one limiting belief, but be sure to only try and tackle them one at a time!

HIGHLIGHT IT TO THE CLIENT

Once you've heard it, it is important for us to bring the limiting belief to our client's attention, as the chances are, they are not aware it exists. Or rather, they may see it as a fact as opposed to a belief.

We can do this simply by finding a way to repeat the statement back to our clients so that they are fully aware that they said it.

Something along the lines of:

> *"I heard you say that you don't believe that you are smart enough to do this, is that how you feel?"*

CHALLENGE

Next up, we want to challenge that belief with questions designed to make your client question the foundations on which it has been formed.

Let's say that the limiting belief you identify is that your client believes they can't start their own business because they are not smart enough.

Some challenging questions we could use for our above example include:

- *Who told you that you aren't smart enough?*
- *What's the smartest thing you've ever done?*
- *What does smart mean?*
- *Just how smart is 'enough'?*
- *What attributes do you have which could build a business?*
- *What is un-true about what you've just said?*

TAKING ACTION TO START A POSITIVE BELIEF CYCLE

Finally, we need to encourage our client to start taking action to prove that this limiting belief is not the undisputed factual statement they think it is.

This will help them to break their current 'Belief Cycle', as demonstrated by the diagram on the next page, and form a new positive belief cycle.

The Belief & Success Cycle

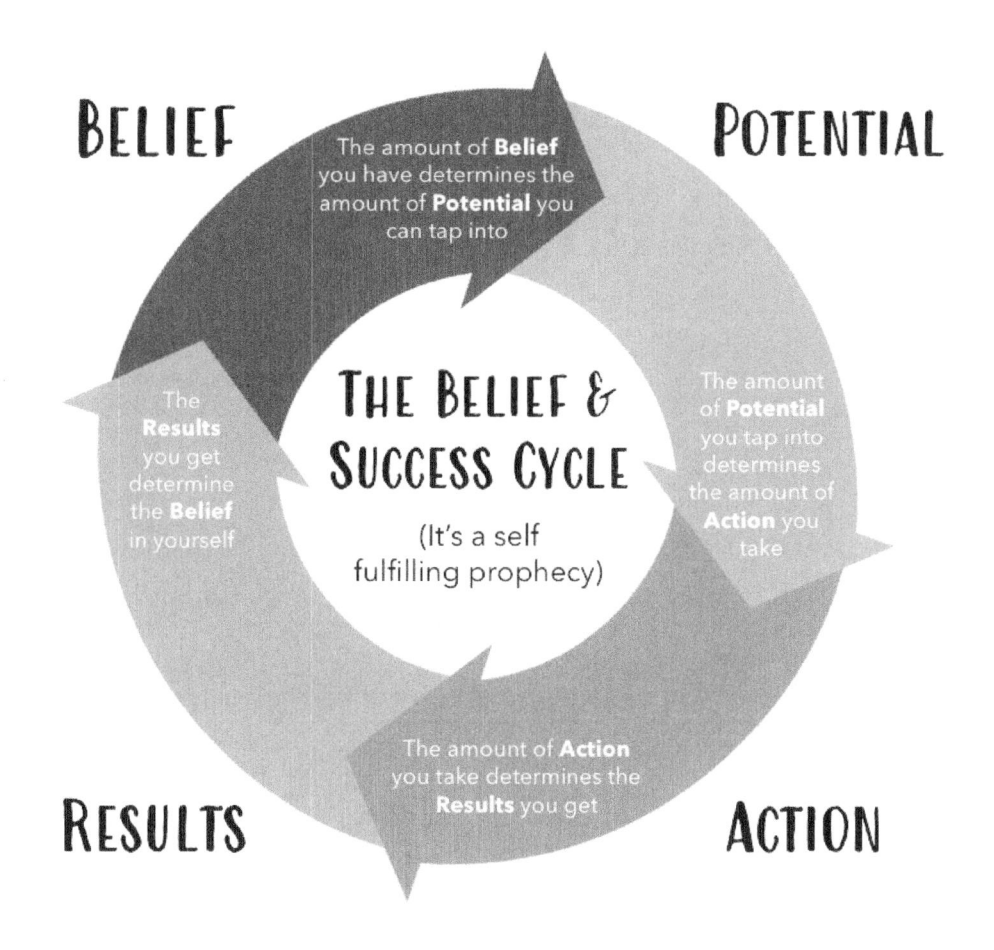

BELIEF
The amount of **Belief** you have determines the amount of **Potential** you can tap into

POTENTIAL
The amount of **Potential** you tap into determines the amount of **Action** you take

ACTION
The amount of **Action** you take determines the **Results** you get

RESULTS
The **Results** you get determine the **Belief** in yourself

(It's a self fulfilling prophecy)

No matter how small the action your client takes is, it should still help. As Dr Martin Luther King Jr said: *"Take the first step in faith. You don't have to see the whole staircase, just take the first step"*

C is for Circle of Influence

The Circle of Influence is a quick and easy tool created by Stephen Covey, author of *'The 7 Habits of Highly Effective People'*.[8]

In his well renowned book, Covey wrote:

> *"Instead of reacting to or worrying about conditions over which they have little or no control, proactive people focus their time and energy on things they can control. The problems, challenges, and opportunities we face fall into two areas—Circle of Concern and Circle of Influence"*

The 'Circle of Influence' exercise works best for clients who are feeling overwhelmed by various issues all at once, or for clients who are presenting as feeling out of control or hopeless.

Just follow these simple steps:

1. Have your client write out a list of all their current concerns, challenges and issues that they are facing.

2. Have your client draw out a series of circles like the below diagram and label the circles as follows:

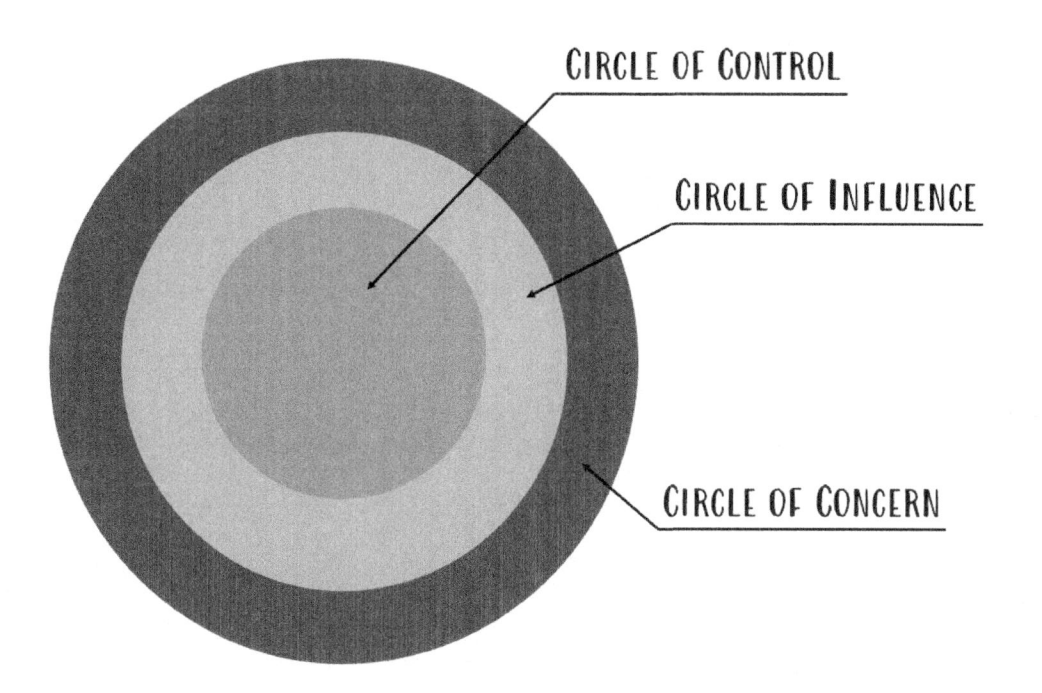

CIRCLE OF CONTROL

CIRCLE OF INFLUENCE

CIRCLE OF CONCERN

3. Ask your client to separate their list of issues into the following three areas and write them down in the corresponding circle. So:

   - Issues that they can control and therefore do something about (e.g. their fitness level) would sit inside the 'Circle of Control'.

- Issues that they can influence (e.g. other people's behaviour) would sit inside the 'Circle of Influence'.
- Issues they cannot control or influence (e.g. their past decisions or being made redundant) would sit inside the 'Circle of Concern'.

The benefit of running through this exercise is for your client to learn how to prioritise more effectively, set achievable goals and minimise the amount of energy that they waste fretting over things they cannot change.

The idea is not to do this exercise just once and then forget about it, but to encourage your client to get into the habit of, when dealing with different situations or challenges, start thinking to themselves *"Is this within my circle of influence or control, or is it only in my circle of concern?"*

D is for Delving Deeper

An easy trap to fall into when you are coaching is to focus purely on the problems and challenges that the client brings to your sessions. Of course, it is understandable to want to explore these too, but often if you stay focused on purely what they have presented to you, the coaching will feel like it is going around in circles and the client won't gain any new awareness that will help them avoid similar problems in the future.

Delving deeper into what is underneath the often surface-level issues that clients present us with can be uncomfortable. You might be wary of their emotional reaction, or of the awkwardness that may follow. But much of the value in coaching is being able to push past the surface and get to the root cause.

As coaches we must spend more time on uncovering our clients fears, beliefs, assumptions and conflicts of values. Often, in trying to achieve this, there will be times where it seems as if your client has hit a metaphorical wall. This is normal, as most of us spend little to no time examining the things that you will be asking. They may respond with "I don't know". At that point it is important not to give up, but to gently encourage them to dig deeper within themselves to search for the answer.

So how can we do this?

Well a few questions you might like to use, depending on the context of course, include:

- *What is it about this question (or issue) that makes it difficult to answer (or painful)?*
- *How would other people, whose opinions you value, see this?*
- *What do you want to know about this and what would you rather not know?*
- *What would you say right now if you did know?*

Another good tip for ensuring that you are digging deep enough is to ensure you ask "And what else?" after initially asking a client what it is they want, or what is on their mind, for example. As I've mentioned, often what they present initially is not the full picture and by responding in a way that politely implies: that answer wasn't good enough, try again, they are forced to look internally for more.

Too many coaching engagements fail because the coach fails to drill down to the underlying coaching need. Often the presenting symptoms are not the real problem.

E is for Exploring Change

There are many reasons why an individual may seek out a coach. Perhaps they're feeling unfulfilled and they want some clarity, perhaps they're looking to improve their confidence, or perhaps they're having a hard time achieving their goals. Whatever the reason is, the chances are that if they are going to make real progress, they are going to need to make some real changes.

There is a model I learnt about during my training called 'The Neurological Levels of Change' (sometimes also referred to as the 'Logical Levels') by an organizational psychologist named Robert Dilts[9]. This model is part of the theory that for sustainable change to be made, it needs to occur and be supported by, changes in more than one 'level'.

THE NEUROLOGICAL LEVELS OF CHANGE:

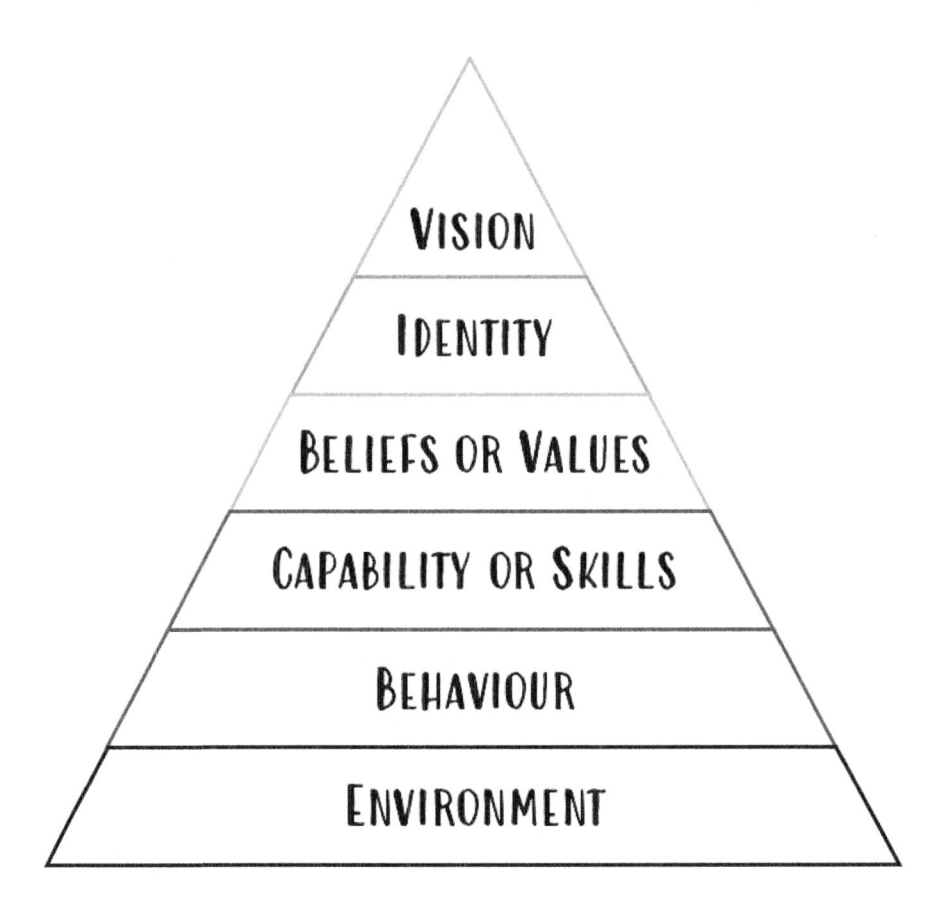

```
        VISION
       IDENTITY
    BELIEFS OR VALUES
   CAPABILITY OR SKILLS
       BEHAVIOUR
       ENVIRONMENT
```

Dilts concluded that when change occurs at a lower level only, it is unlikely to be sustained. Old habits die hard after all...

Let's start by looking at what each of the layers really mean[10].

The base layer is **Environment.** This is where you are and what is around you. It includes where you work, where you live and the people there too.

Next up is **Behaviour.** This is what you actually do, which of course takes place within your environment.

Continuing up we have **Capability.** This refers to what you are able to do and the skills that you have. Your behaviour is chosen from within your range of skills.

Then we have **Beliefs/Values**. This refers to what is important to you. What you believe about yourself, about others and about the world in general. Your beliefs and values motivate you.

Above this we have **Identity.** This is all about your sense of self.

Finally we have **Vision.** This is about what you are a part of that is more important tot you than you are to yourself. What do you feel connected to? For some people this refers to religion, spirituality, family or indeed there may be a gap there.

If we examine the theory that change needs to happen at multiple levels to be maintained by looking at an example:

A colleague goes on a management skills course and learns some new management techniques. They come back and implement them for a while, but then they slowly slip back into old habits.

Dilts would argue that is because they've learned new skills (capability level) but their values, beliefs and sense of identity that govern whether they use those skills did not change. Deep down, for whatever reason, the new skills were not important enough to them, or they didn't feel like they fitted with their view of themselves, and therefore the change was not sustainable.

In terms of how we use this in our coaching, it's important to listen to the client's use of language:

- I usually end up in the kitchen at parties (environment/behaviour)
- I argue a lot (behaviour)
- I'm not very good at sports (capability)
- People shouldn't lie (belief)
- I want to be less stressed (value)
- That's just the sort of person I am (identity)

You may notice your client is focusing around certain levels – you can gather more information by asking questions that take them to other levels. For example:

- What do you feel when that happens? (behaviour)
- Why is that important to you? (value)
- What assumptions are you making about this? (belief)
- What does that say about you as a person? (identity)
- What does that do for you? (value)

Human beings have a tendency to only really make changes at the Environment or Behaviour levels, which is often why we don't keep them up.

You want to try and encourage your clients to make changes significantly high up enough in the pyramid for it to stick. This can be called a 'top-down' approach.

For example, let's say your client is very disorganised and wants to become more organised and able to multi-task. Instead of just focusing on helping them to changing their behaviour, we want to work with them to make a change at the upper levels, as this should change everything below it in order to support the higher-level change. If we work with them on the level of Identity and try to shift their view of themselves as a disorganised person to an efficient and successful person instead, then their beliefs, capabilities and behaviour should also be modified as a result.

F is for the FEAR Model

Fear is a natural, emotional response that we all have, induced by a perceived threat of some kind. It is there to protect us from danger.

Have you ever been fearful of something and felt it spread throughout your entire body? Most people have. Fear can have a really dramatic physical and emotional effect on people.

There are lots of different fears out there, but here is a list of some of the most common fears that may arise in coaching:

- Fear of failure
- Fear of embarrassment
- Fear of rejection
- Fear of intimacy
- Fear of the unknown

One of our roles as coaches is to try and help our clients overcome their fears. It is part of our job to help our clients move forward and make progress in their lives, and if fear is standing in their way then it's going to hinder this process.

We must try to help them tackle, embrace and breakdown their fear, and we can do this by using this handy FEAR Model[11]:

F – Find
E – Embrace
A – Action
R – Review

FIND

In order to remove fear we must first find it. When someone is scared of something, they probably won't want to spend much time thinking about it or focusing on it because it's not particularly enjoyable for them to do so. But it is our job to gently coax the fear to the surface so that we can begin to work through it with the client.

There are various ways you can do this. As a first port of call try and get your client to discuss the fear with you and break down exactly what it is that they are afraid of. If you think it may be helpful to the client then you could also get them to write about the fear or draw the fear.

Here are some questions to help you coax the fear out:

- *What comes up for you around the word 'fear'?*
- *What is it that you are specifically scared of?*
- *When (or where) would this fear tend to come up for you?*

EMBRACE

This stage involves your client vividly imagining and accepting what would happen if their fear was to become a reality. This is designed to weaken the fear.

Ask your client questions like:

- *What is the worst-case scenario here?*
- *Okay we've heard about the worst case, but what is likely to happen?*
- *How would facing this fear help you to grow?*
- *What would you gain from letting this fear go?*
- *How would it feel to no longer have the fear in your life?*

ACTION

Now you need to gently encourage your client to take some form of action in order to work towards eliminating the fear. This may be daunting for them at first but try and get them to see how it is holding them back and what can be gained by letting it go.

Ask your client questions like:

- *How do you intend to face this fear?*
- *When?*
- *How will you know when you've faced it?*

REVIEW

Finally, once your client has taken a step toward facing their fear in some capacity, it is important to invite them to tell you about their experience doing so.

Essentially you want them to recognise that through action they have managed to, as a minimum, reduce the fear significantly. This can be done by reviewing the process and giving them the space to talk about their experience.

Hopefully the more they do this the smaller the fear will get as they begin to feel empowered and proud of themselves.

G is for the GROW Model

The GROW model is a simple, yet effective framework for structuring your coaching sessions. It is one of the most well renowned coaching models out there, and will serve you very well, time after time.

The original acronym, as invented by business coaches Graham Alexander, Alan Fine and Sir John Whitmore[12] back in the 1980's stands for:

G – Goals
R – Reality
O – Options
W – Way forward

However, I do also use a modified version of the acronym in my coaching work as well:

G – Grows
R – *Resources*
O – *Obstacles*
W – Way forward

The original model should be your go-to, but the second version also has its benefits. I would invite you to try both, as I do.

The first port of call in both models is to uncover what the client's **Goal** is. Goals should be SMART wherever possible (specific, measurable, achievable, realistic and time specific). To ensure that your client is thinking 'smartly' you may want to ask questions such as *"How will you know when you've achieved this goal?"*

Next up traditionally would be **Reality**. That is, to examine the current reality for your client. Simply ask them to describe what is happening now, and as they do so the solution may even begin to emerge. Too often people try to reach a goal without giving much thought to their starting position.

In the second version of the acronym you would now look at what **Resources** are available to the client to help them with their goal. A lot of the time we give little thought to what is out there that can help us to achieve our goals. It is worth encouraging your client to think about a mixture of both external and internal resources. An internal resource would be things like 'drive' or 'ambition'. Or, if your client presented with a dream of setting up their own travel business, then an internal resource could be the fact that they were bilingual! External resources include considerations such as access to certain information or useful contacts, or a type of software programme they have access to.

You can ask Resource-focused questions such as:

- *What internal resources do you have that will help you achieve this goal, and which might you need to develop?*
- *What external resources do you have that will help you achieve this goal, and which might you need to develop?*
- *What resources have you not thought of yet?*
- *Where could you obtain these resources?*
- *Who else could help you achieve this goal?*

Next up is **Options.** Once your client has explored their current reality, it's time for them to start brainstorming what the options are for reaching their goal.

Let them sit with this for as long as it takes for them to explore the different options available. You may want to use the following questions to try and ensure the client is really thinking it through from all angles:

- *What else could you do?*
- *What are the advantages and disadvantages of each option?*

- *If X or Y constraint was removed, would that change things?*

If we're combining both models, then you would also want to use this time to cover **Obstacles**. It's important that the client thinks through the obstacles that they may face when trying to achieve their goal - forewarned is forearmed after all.

- *What obstacles might you encounter when pursuing this goal?*
- *What is stopping you from achieving this goal?*
- *What do you need to stop doing in order to achieve your goal?*
- *What mind-set barrier may you face and what can you do to work on this?*

Finally, both models agree that we must now round off by focusing on the client's **Way Forward.** You want the client to commit to taking specific actions in order to move them closer towards their goal. By doing this you will help them to establish their will and hopefully boost their motivation and drive.

Ask questions like:

- *Tell me how you're going to make this goal a reality?*
- *What are you going to do today to achieve this goal?*
- *What are three actions you can take that would make sense this week?*
- *What actionable step do you need to take to ensure you're successful with this goal?*

Finally, I would encourage client and coach to both decide on a date where you will review the client's progress. This provides a level of 'accountability' which is vital.

H is for Homework

The term 'homework' can have negative connotations for some, but it is undeniably a highly useful element of the coaching process.

If you are working with a client who has only signed up for a six-week coaching programme, for example, then there is only so much progress they can make within that time. However, if you are also able to set them 'coaching homework' in between sessions, then you improve their chances of reaching their goals.

Coaching homework can take many different forms. It may come in the form of a self-reflection exercise, an experiment to try or a writing task. Of course, the type of homework you set your client will vary according to the type of coaching you are doing. For example, if you are specialising in career coaching then the homework you set may be related to them identifying their workplace skills and strengths.

Setting homework has several benefits. Firstly, as I mentioned before, it should take your client further toward achieving their goals (providing you have worked with your client in order to establish what sorts of behaviours and experiences are likely to facilitate goal achievement). Secondly, it can be used to ensure that your client has properly absorbed and understood what you have discussed in your session together. And thirdly, it encourages independence and self-motivation, and can help your client to develop positive habits.

Here are some examples of homework tasks you might want to consider

- Letter writing exercises (to past you or future you, for example)
- Journaling (we look at this in more detail in a later chapter)
- Writing lists
- Practicing positive affirmations
- Identifying negative thought patterns by keeping a Thought Tracker
- Completing online assessments such as 'Strengths Finder' to develop self-knowledge and awareness

It is worth mentioning that if your client seems to fall into the category of people who recoil at the term 'homework' then it is best avoided. You will know your client best, so you can decide whether to label the tasks you set with a different label (perhaps 'action' or 'assignment') or to not use any label at all.

I is for Initial Call (or Discovery Call)

The first interaction you have with a prospective client can be referred to as an 'Initial Call' or 'Discovery Call'. The focus of this first communication should be on discovering information about the client and their reasons for wanting a coach.

This initial conversation between the coach and the potential client is vitally important for a number of reasons. From the client's side, this is the stage where they find out how you like to work, what you charge, and how it all works. This information will help to determine whether they feel you are the right fit for them. Equally, from your side as the coach, this is your opportunity to get a feel for the client, to see what their motivation is for entering a coaching relationship and whether they are truly open to the process.

Effectively what is happening at this stage in the coaching relationship is that you are both getting to know each other and seeing if you are compatible to work together moving forward.

Before you even have the call, think about what you can do to ensure you are in the right headspace for it. For some people this may mean sitting in meditation for a few minutes beforehand or going for a run or doing yoga. For others it might mean repeating a couple of positive affirmations. Whatever you need to do to ensure you are feeling your best, make time for it just before your call.

Here is a brief outline or a 10-step process that you can use for the actual call with a potential client. Please remember that this is **not** a coaching session at this stage.

1. **Make a connection**
   "I'm really pleased to meet you" (or speak to you if this is on the phone!)
   "Is it alright if I ask you some questions to get to know you and your situation a bit better?"

2. **Get a brief overview of where they are at the moment**
   "Tell me a bit about your life"
   "What's going on for you at the moment?"

3. **Uncover what it is they want most**
   "If you could have everything you want in your life, what would that look and feel like?"

4. **Help them to emotionally connect to this vision**
   "What would achieving this dream/goal mean to you?"
   "How important would you say it is on a scale of 1-10?"

5. **Ask them what is standing in their way**
   "What is stopping you from having this?"

6. **Help them to realise the cost of living with the status quo**
   "What impact has this had on you?"
   "What has it cost you?"

7. **Show them the bigger why**
   "If you could overcome this, what would that do for you?"

8. **Gather the gems**
   "What have you taken from this conversation so far?"

9. **Invite them in for a proper session**
   *"Are you ready to let me help you to achieve *insert goal*?*

10. **Share your contract and terms with them**
    This is where you either email or physically give them your welcome pack, which should contain your contract terms, along with details of fees etc.

The above can and should be elaborated on of course, but the most important point to remember is that we want the potential client to finish the call feeling positive about the future and motivated to start the coaching process with you.

J is for Journaling

One coaching tool that I would highly recommend suggesting to your client early on is that of journaling.

I like to invite my clients to keep a journal throughout their coaching journey with me (and ideally beyond as well).

The main benefit for doing so is that journaling requires introspection, and introspection can often lead to making changes.

The other benefits of keeping a journal can be explained with this handy JOURNAL acronym[13] that you may wish to share with your client:

- **J – Judgement Free**
  It's important to encourage your client to write what is in their heart. The journal is a private, safe space for them to express their thoughts and feelings away from the judgement of others.

- **O – Observation**

    Explain that this is a great opportunity for the client to step into an 'observing' role. Encourage them to write down their experiences and then to reflect and interpret them accordingly.

- **U – Understanding**

    By the client observing their experiences, this will hopefully lead to better understanding. When we understand our thought patterns and behaviours better, it can lead to us being able to manage them more effectively.

- **R – Revelation**

    Journaling can often lead to revelations about what it is we actually want. Our hopes, dreams, goals and aspirations – it can help us to get in touch with our core selves.

- **N – Needs Assessment**

    By keeping a regular journal the client is more likely to pick up on what the problems and potential solutions may be in their lives. Writing things down often results in more clarity.

- **A – Awareness**

    Writing things down also enables your client to gain a wider perspective on their life. It can remind them where the problem areas are, but also what to be grateful for. Awareness is necessary in order to start to make changes and also to appreciate what they already have.

- **L – Life**
   It's been proven that journaling can decrease stress levels and anxiety. Even if its just for a few minutes a day it can improve your client's quality of life.

Hopefully after running through the reasoning behind journaling, your client will be willing to give it a go. By introducing this as an element to your coaching, you are holding your client accountable to documentation as well as enabling them to monitor their own progress.

Make sure to check in with your client and ask how their journaling is going in future sessions. It should bring them a greater level of awareness and mindfulness.

K is for Key Coaching Skills

As well as the use of coaching models and frameworks, there are several important key skills that coaches should be demonstrating in each of their client sessions.

Key skills:

- Listening
- Questioning
- Reflecting
- Challenging

LISTENING

Having highly developed listening skills is a core requirement of being a coach[14]. It sounds obvious, but there is a lot more to the skill of listening than meets the eye (or the ear).

Listening is something we all tend to feel we do well at, but like any form of skill it needs to be practiced and developed to get the best from it. Stephen Covey, author of *The 7 Habits of Highly Effective People* who I mentioned in an earlier chapter, once said: *"Most people do not listen with the intent to understand; they listen with the intent to reply."* This can be an easy trap to fall into, especially at the beginning of your coaching career whilst you build up your familiarity with the process and your confidence as a coach.

Effective listening requires concentration and a focused effort that is known as 'active listening', which is a term coined by Carl Rogers and Richard Farson back in 1957[15]. Today, the International Coaching Federation includes active listening as a core competency[16], describing it as:

> *"The ability to focus completely on what the client is saying and is not saying, to understand the meaning of what is said in the context of the client's desires and to support client self-expression."*

Features of active listening often include:

- Presenting as neutral and non-judgmental
- Giving verbal and non-verbal feedback to show that you are listening, for example leaning in, mirroring body language, eye contact and smiling
- Not filling silences and staying patient
- Reflecting back what has been said (more on this later)
- Asking clarifying questions (more on this later)

But as well as a potential lack of confidence early on in your coaching career, there are several other barriers that can hinder effective and active listening. These include:

- Distractions in your physical environment
- Excess internal dialogue and mental distractions
- Content overload
- Boredom and 'pseudo listening'
- Assumptions by the coach
- Defensive listening (when you are disagreeing with what the client is saying inside your head)

Unfortunately, these barriers can be quite detrimental to the coaching process, so here are five simple tips that you can use to overcome barriers to active listening:

1. Prepare beforehand. Set time aside ahead of your coaching session and clear your mind in readiness. Ensure that your physical environment is free from distractions wherever possible

2. Learn to understand what internal dialogue is occurring within you; are there any triggers or themes?

3. Learn to create good notes, keep them succinct and meaningful so that you can refer back to them

4. Resist mental distractions – when you feel your listening veer off bring it back

5. Hear your client out before you step in. Don't judge or interrupt them, just listen

Through active listening, you will be able to accurately reflect back to your client what's been said and show that you've been listening—not just hearing—and that you genuinely understand the feeling/s or message/s they are trying to convey. This will help to create an environment that allows for them to go deeper and come to new realisations, and is the basis for trust and respect in the coach/client relationship.

QUESTIONING

Effective questioning is crucial for successful coaching. It allows the coach to get to grips with the issues, and the client to verbalise previously unconsidered thoughts or feelings, which promotes reflection. Effective questions help get to the heart of the issue and can help facilitate change.

In terms of what constitutes an effective question, coaches should be trying to focus on asking open, probing questions which seek clarification. On occasion, there may also be benefit in asking hypothetical questions, which don't necessarily demand actual answers but work to provoke reflective thought in our clients.

This is not to say that we as coaches should get fixated on asking a string of questions for the sake of doing so, instead we need to listen to what our client is saying and only ask the questions that are carefully considered, clear, concise, relevant, and most importantly, designed to encourage our clients to dig deeper to find the answers that will help them to move forward.

Let us quickly look at some of the different terminology regarding question types[17]:

OPEN QUESTIONS VS CLOSED QUESTIONS

As I've mentioned above, a question is much more effective when it encourages your client to reflect and elaborate. In order for us to do this as coaches, we want to focus on asking open questions and avoid asking closed questions as much as possible.

To explain the difference, if you asked, for example: "Do you enjoy working as a nurse?" this has the potential to stop the conversation with just a "Yes" or a "No" answer. Therefore, it is a *closed-ended* question.

However, if you changed that question to: "What about working as a nurse is satisfying to you?" then you are likely to get far more engagement from your client, as it is an *open-ended* question. Notice that it begins with one of the 5 W's (who, what, where, when, and why), which is often the case for open-ended questions.

PROBING QUESTIONS

Probing can be defined as inquiring closely into something and indeed, probing questions in coaching are designed to do just that. A client may share something with you that you think may benefit further exploration and this is when you might ask a probing question in order to find out more detail and/or to help the client think more deeply about whatever it is they are discussing.

Some examples of probing questions include:

- *Why do you think this is the case?*
- *What do you think would happen if...?*
- *What sort of impact do you think...?*
- *How did you decide...?*
- *How did you conclude...?*

CLARIFYING QUESTIONS

Clarifying questions are simple questions of fact, that are designed to reassure the speaker that you are listening to them and attempting to understand the messages that they are expressing.

This is very useful in coaching and helps to build rapport and empathic understanding between the coach and the client.

Here are a few examples of Clarifying Questions:

- *Did I hear you say...?*
- *Did I understand you when you said...?*
- *Can I ask what you meant when you said...?*
- *Did I hear you correctly when you said...?*

10 OF MY FAVOURITE COACHING QUESTIONS

Here is a list of 10 questions that I particularly enjoy asking in my coaching work. I find that they often provoke deep discussion and can take the client by surprise. If they are not your cup of tea, that's absolutely fine, there is no right or wrong question to ask in coaching. I just personally have found them to be quite powerful questions to ask.

1. *What are you unclear about in your life, that if you figured it out, would make the biggest difference?*

2. *What is standing in your way?*

3. *What would you do if you were 10 times bolder?*

4. *Who do you want to become?*

5. *What changes do you need to make to have the life you want?*

6. *What do you like about yourself (interests, life experiences, personality traits, etc.)?*

7. *What is the deeper meaning or personal significance that this goal has for you?*

8. *What is your definition of success?*

9. *What will happen if you don't take this step?*

10. *What is the most important thing in the world to you? And why?*

While asking questions is a core part of coaching, remember that if you don't have the right question to ask in the moment, it is okay not to ask one. It's important to be comfortable with silence too.

REFLECTING

As the name would suggest, reflecting refers to the art of reflecting back the words, thoughts and feelings that you have picked up from your client.

In terms of the benefit this serves to the coaching process, effective reflecting shows that you are listening, which in turn helps you to build rapport with your client.

It also helps your client to hear what they have just said, which sounds obvious, but can be quite powerful for the client and often prompts further exploration.

The two main techniques within reflecting are 'mirroring' and 'paraphrasing'.

Mirroring is a simple form of reflecting and quite literally involves repeating almost exactly what your client has said. It should be short and simple – it is usually sufficient to just repeat the key words or the last few words spoken. It shows your client that you are trying to understand their terms of reference and also acts as a prompt for them to continue speaking. Mirroring should not be overused as this can become annoying and therefore detract from the ultimate aim of building rapport.

Paraphrasing involves using words other than those that your client has said in order to reflect what they meant. It shows not only that you were listening, but that you are attempting to understand what they are saying. To paraphrase effectively, it is important not to introduce your own ideas or question the client's thoughts/feelings/actions. Your responses need to be impartial and non-judgemental.

When this technique is first used it can seem stilted and unnatural but as you practice and become more comfortable using it, you will hopefully come to see its benefits.

CHALLENGING

As Fred DeVito once said: *"If it doesn't challenge you, it doesn't change you".*

I believe there is a lot of truth in that, and being able to challenge effectively is one of the key skills any coach needs to possess.

However, it is important to master how to do this in a non-confrontational manner, so as not to offend or alienate your client.

Challenging is about not accepting whatever it is your client has said just at face value. It is about stretching your client, be that through setting them a task that takes them beyond their usual self-imposed limits, or by questioning their beliefs, actions or inconsistencies in what they are saying.

The aim of using challenging questions is for your client to pause, reflect and explain. They may end up adopting an alternative viewpoint or they may not, but either way the process is a beneficial one as it will hopefully raise their own self-awareness.

Here are a couple of examples of using challenging questions in coaching practice:

> *"Just now you mentioned that you wanted to start running again...although in your last session you said that you didn't really enjoy running...tell me what the truth is here?'*

> *"You have said that in order to be a good parent you cannot leave them for any time with a babysitter. Where has this belief come from?"*

You can also literally set challenges for your client if you feel it will help move them forward, so for example, when dealing with a client who is overwhelmed with demands and struggles with people pleasing:

> *"I challenge you to say "no" to anything that is not a priority this week"*

Using challenging skills within coaching should always be done with empathy and understanding. You must use your own judgement of your client and your coaching relationship as to how much or how little to incorporate it into your sessions.

If you master these key skills then your coaching sessions will be all the more effective for doing so.

L is for Language

Language is central to how we communicate and how we understand, or seek to be understood. It gives us the ability to formulate, express and communicate our thoughts. It also structures our entire world and the meaning and associations of words.

Within coaching, and specifically NLP coaching (which we will touch on more later in this book), it is believed that by altering the way different words and associations shape a person's network of vocabularies, you can begin to change the way they think and perceive the world around them.

For example, think of the word 'failure' – what does this mean to you?

To some, the word may represent extreme disappointment, sadness and trigger the sinking sensation in the stomach. These associations may alter how they will react to a failure - or risk of failure - in the future. However, others may associate the word with new beginnings, a fresh start and another life experience.

There are two main language models in NLP coaching which are known as: 'Meta Model' and 'Milton Model'. In this chapter, I shall be focusing on the Meta Model and how to use it in coaching interactions.

THE META MODEL[18]

The Meta Model is based upon the notion that we don't operate on the world directly but that instead we take in information through our sense organs and then use three processes known as 'distortions', 'deletions' and 'generalisations' to form an internal representation in our minds. This internal representation is often referred to in NLP as 'our map' and it is made up of pictures, feelings, sounds, tastes and smells. NLP says that the maps we make in our minds are not the world itself but rather our individual internal representations of it.

Let's have a look at the 3 processes we filter information through:

1. DELETIONS

Deletion is the process of selective attention. Whether this be a conscious decision or an unconscious process, it is clearly impossible to pay attention to the mass of information that impacts our senses. At some level of awareness, you have to choose what to pay attention to. By choosing to focus on some aspect of your sensory experience, you naturally have to delete other information. An example of this might be how, to hear someone in a crowded room you may have to concentrate in on the speaker and not listen to the other conversations going on. Driving a car in heavy traffic you may need to focus on the road ahead to the detriment of the scenery that passes you by. At times deletion may be useful yet in other contexts it may result in a negative experience. For example, if you delete the nice things that people say to you and do for you, and instead focus on what they did not do or say then you may feel unloved.

2. DISTORTIONS

Distortion is the process by which you construct, manufacture, create and manipulate sensory data. It is the process of bringing in information through your senses and then playing with that information in your mind to create new concepts, ideas and understandings. Different ways of thinking about the world, philosophy, spirituality, religion, ideology, fantasising about a lover, creating new inventions, writing fiction and producing films all rely upon the ability to distort so called 'reality'.

3. GENERALISATIONS

Generalisation is the process of taking an individual experience and turning it into universals. For example, if an individual has a bad experience with a dog as a child, they may then conclude that all dogs are dangerous. When people create these types of generalisations it may limit rather than enhance their lives.

The Meta Model is a set of language patterns that reconnects these deletions, distortions and generalisations that occur in everyday language use, with the experience that generated them.

If you turn over the page, you will find a table that gives you an overview of the different language patterns and examples of where they may occur in a coaching setting, along with how you can respond in order to challenge your client to explore and expand further.

PATTERN NAME	MEANING	EXAMPLE (client)
Nominalisation	When you turn a non-physical item into a physical item.	"There is awful **communication** in this house"
Unspecified Verb	Verb = Describes an action. The problem is where the action is not being explained.	"He **rejected** me"
Simple Deletion	So much missing information!	"I'm uncomfortable" "I don't like working out"
Lack of Referential Index	Vague terms are used in place of specific detail.	"**They** don't listen to me" "I don't agree with **that**"
Comparative Deletions	Comparing something to nothing.	"She is **better than** me" "That car is **too expensive**"

DELETIONS

HOW DO YOU KNOW WHEN ITS HAPPENING?	HOW THE COACH RESPONDS
The Wheelbarrow test. If you can't put it in a wheelbarrow, then it is a nominalisation.	"What specifically do you mean by communication?"
Your client will state an action without giving any details around HOW it's happened.	"How specifically did he reject you?" "What do you mean by rejection?"
Your client will leave blanks that need to be filled in to make perfect sense of the sentence.	"What specifically are you uncomfortable about?" "What specific part of working out do you not like?"
Your client will group people together "They won't like me", "Employers don't like too many jobs on a resume", "Men don't like smart women".	"Who specially are they?" "What exactly don't you agree with?"
Vague comparisons use words like better, faster, stronger, improved, more, less, very, bigger, smaller, healthier, superior, smarter, enhanced. Marketers love these terms in commercials and advertisements.	"Better how?" "Expensive compared to what?"

PATTERN NAME	MEANING	EXAMPLE (client)
		DISTORTI
Mindread	Claiming to know someone's internal state.	"I **know** she doesn't like me"
Lost Performative	Value judgements where the person who is doing the judging is left out.	"It's **bad** to be late" "It's **very important** to dress well"
Cause & Effect	Where cause is put wrongly out of self.	"He **makes me** angry" "When she yells, **I get** upset"
Complex Equivalent	Where two experiences are interpreted as being synonymous.	"She shouts at me, so I know she hates me" "He is always late from work so he must be cheating on me"
Presuppositions	Assuming something to be true without facts.	"If my husband knew how much I suffered, he wouldn't do that"

HOW DO YOU KNOW WHEN ITS HAPPENING?	HOW THE COACH RESPONDS
ONS	
When you would need to be a mind reader to actually know this to be fact.	"How specifically do you know she doesn't like you?"
Your client will make a judgement, but you don't know who is doing the judging.	"Who says it's bad to be late?" "According to whom is it important?"
Your client will state that A = B. "This" will result in "That".	"How specifically does he make you angry?" "How specifically does her yelling allow you to feel upset?"
Your client will describe two completely separate experiences as being directly linked.	"What else could the shouting mean?" "Is it possible that he is genuinely late?"
Your client will be guessing someone else's opinion or actions	"How do you choose to suffer?" "How is he (re)acting?" "How do you know he doesn't know?"

PATTERN NAME	MEANING	EXAMPLE (client)
Universal Quantifier	Words that group all possibilities together.	"She will **never** listen to me"
Modal Operators of Necessity	Words such as should, must, have to, need to.	"I **shouldn't** be thinking this way"
Modal Operators of Possibility	Words such as can, will, may, possible.	"I **can't** tell him the truth"

HOW DO YOU KNOW WHEN ITS HAPPENING?	HOW THE COACH RESPONDS
GENERALISATIONS	
Your client will use generalisations like all, every, never, everyone, no-one.	The best way to challenge a universal quantifier is to say the word back as a question. E.g. "NEVER?"
Your client will use generalisations like should/shouldn't, must/mustn't, have to/don't have to, need to/don't need to.	"What would happen if you did?" "What would happen if you didn't?"
Your client will use generalisations like can/can't, will/won't, may/may not, possible/impossible.	"What would happen if you did?" "What would happen if you didn't?"

I would encourage you to pick one Meta-Model example from the table above and spend the whole day listening out for it when speaking to people. When you hear it, politely challenge it as per the column on the far right and see how it impacts the conversation.

If as coaches, we can harness the power of language, then we can use it to help our clients break down the mental barriers that they unknowingly create for themselves.

M is for MBTI

MBTI stands for Myers-Briggs Type Indicator and is a well-known personality-profiling tool. While MBTI has had its share of critics, it is undeniably a very widely used tool that has been researched and refined over decades, and whilst there are several other personality-profiling models out there, this is the one that I personally find most useful.

Based on Swiss psychiatrist Carl Jung's theory of psychological types, MBTI was developed by an American mother (Katherine Briggs) and daughter (Isabel Myers)[19]. The MBTI simplifies Jung's theory and indicates eight personality preferences, made up of the following four pair groups:

Extraversion (E) – Introversion (I)
Sensing (S) – Intuition (N)
Thinking (T) – Feeling (F)
Judging (J) – Perceiving (P)

In order to work out your preferences, you must undertake the MBTI questionnaire, which will allocate you one of 16 personality types based on how your answers relate to the following key questions:

- Where you focus your attention – Extraversion (E) or Introversion (I)
- The way you take in information – Sensing (S) or INtuition (N)
- How you make decisions – Thinking (T) or Feeling (F)
- How you deal with the world – Judging (J) or Perceiving (P)

After identifying your preferences within the pair groups mentioned above, you end up with a four-letter code, representing your type. Mine, for example, is ENFJ. This means that my preferences are Extraversion, Intuition, Feeling and Judging.

Here is a table to illustrate the different preferences in more detail:

TYPE PREFERENCES

Where you focus your attention	**E**	**Extraversion** People who prefer Extraversion tend to focus their attention on the outer world of people and things.	**I**	**Introversion** People who prefer Introversion tend to focus their attention on the inner world of ideas and impressions.
The way you take in information	**S**	**Sensing** People who prefer Sensing tend to take in information through the five sense and focus on the here and now.	**N**	**Intuition** People who prefer Intuition tend to take in information from patterns and the big picture and focus on future possibilities.
The way you make decisions	**T**	**Thinking** People who prefer Thinking tend to make decisions based primarily on logic and on objective analysis of cause and effect.	**F**	**Feeling** People who prefer Feeling tend to make decisions based primarily on values and on subjective evaluation of person-centred concerns.
How you deal with the outer world	**J**	**Judging** People who prefer Judging tend to like a planned and organised approach to life and prefer to have things settled.	**P**	**Perceiving** People who prefer Perceiving tend to like a flexible and spontaneous approach to life and prefer to keep their options open.

Each of the 16 personality types have their strengths as well as their areas for development.

I believe that it is of equal importance to understand your client's personality type for coaching purposes as to understand your own type.

The benefits for identifying your MBTI type as a coach include:

- You will become more self-aware
- You will be better positioned to promote your unique strengths
- You will be better able to avoid and resolve conflicts
- You will be able to create and maintain cohesive relationships more effectively

By gaining an understanding of your client's MBTI type and what that means, you should be able to:

- Personalise your coaching conversations with your clients, based on their type
- Help your client to uncover their blind spots
- Tailor your coaching interactions to build a trusting relationship
- Help your client to deepen their self-awareness

If you do not already know your MBTI type, I would suggest taking the online test which can be found at **https://www.mbtionline.com/**. The price is a one-off cost of $49.95.

Alternatively, there are free tests on the internet, but I am unable to vouch for their accuracy or quality.

In terms of how you incorporate this into your coaching process, many coaches ask their clients to undertake the test at the beginning of their relationship so that they have a starting point in understanding the client's preferences and can adapt their coaching style accordingly.

Understanding your MBTI type can help in many different areas of life. I've included a list of three common challenges that your clients may be facing and explained how using MBTI can help in each situation.

CHALLENGE 1: LOOKING FOR A CHANGE OF CAREER

Knowing and understanding your MBTI type will help you to identify your preferences and narrow down your job search accordingly. Some types are more creative than others, some are natural leaders while others are not, some types prefer analytical work etc. It can help to reveal the type of work environment that will and won't work for you. Certain personality types, for example introverted types, may be more content in environments with less people or indeed more home-based work.

Below is a brief summary of each personality type with a couple of careers that tend to fit them well. It is by no means an extensive list, as there are hundreds of potential careers that are not mentioned here, but it is designed to give you an idea of the *type* of work that might suit:

INTJ

Creative perfectionists who prefer to do things their own way, INTJs perform well in non-social roles that require them to think theoretically.

Careers that are often deemed a good fit include: investment banker, financial advisor, economist, software developer and executive.

INTP

Independent and creative problem-solvers, INTPs gravitate toward roles that require them to be theoretical and precise.

Careers that are often deemed a good fit include: Computer programmer, financial analyst, architect, economist, professor

ENTJ

Natural leaders who are logical, analytical, and good strategic planners, ENTJs gravitate toward authoritarian roles that require them to be organized and efficient.

Careers that are often deemed a good fit include: Executive, management consultant, lawyer, venture capitalist

ENTP

Enterprising creative people who enjoy new challenges, ENTPs excel in risky roles that require them to be persistent and non-conformist.

Careers that are often deemed a good fit include: Entrepreneur, real estate developer, politician, advertising creative director

INFJ

Thoughtful, creative people driven by firm principles and personal integrity, INFJs do well in behind-the-scenes roles that require them to communicate on a personal level.

Careers that are often deemed a good fit include: HR, therapist, writers, social worker, customer relations

INFP

Sensitive idealists motivated by their deeper personal values, INFPs excel in roles that require them to be compassionate and adaptable.

Careers that are often deemed a good fit include: Graphic designer, editor, physical therapist

ENFJ

People-lovers who are energetic, articulate, and diplomatic, ENFJs excel in cooperative roles that require them to be expressive and logical.

Careers that are often deemed a good fit include: Corporate coach or trainer, sales manager, public relations specialist, HR specialist

ENFP

Curious and confident creative types who see possibilities everywhere, ENFPs perform well in expressive roles that require them to be alert and communicative.

Careers that are often deemed a good fit include: Journalist, advertising creative director, restauranteur, event planner

ISTJ

Hard workers who value their responsibilities and commitments, ISTJs excel in behind-the-scenes roles that require them to be reliable.

Careers that are often deemed a good fit include: Accountant, auditor, chief financial officer, government employee, web development engineer

ISFJ

Modest and determined workers who enjoy helping others, ISFJs do well in roles that require them to provide services to others without being in a position of authority.

Careers that are often deemed a good fit include: Teacher, dentist, customer service representative, librarian

ESTJ

Realists who are quick to make practical decisions, ESTJs perform well in social roles that require them to lead.

Careers that are often deemed a good fit include: Project manager, operations, judge, lawyer

ESFJ

Gregarious traditionalists motivated to help others, ESFJs gravitate toward social roles that require them to care for the well-being of others

Careers that are often deemed a good fit include: Nurse/ healthcare worker, social worker, teacher

ISTP

Straightforward and honest people who prefer action to conversation, ISTPs perform well in utilitarian roles that require them to make use of tools.

Careers that are often deemed a good fit include: Civil engineer, economist, data communications analysis, pilot, physician

ISFP

Warm and sensitive types who like to help people in tangible ways, ISFPs do well in roles that require them to be sympathetic and attentive

Careers that are often deemed a good fit include: physical therapist, designer, landscape architect, massage therapist

ESTP

Pragmatists who love excitement and excel in a crisis, ESTPs excel in high-stakes roles that require them to be resourceful.

Careers that are often deemed a good fit include: Investor, banker, sports coach, entertainment agent

ESFP

Lively and playful people who value common sense, ESFPs gravitate toward roles that require them to be expressive and interact with others.

Careers that are often deemed a good fit include: Actor, interior designer, environmental scientist

This is by no means a comprehensive list as there are hundreds of careers that haven't been mentioned here of course, but it gives you an idea of the themes that come up.

CHALLENGE 2: CONFLICT IN PERSONAL RELATIONSHIPS

Conflict and confrontation is rarely fun, but it is part of how we come to conclusions about things, and sometimes it is even required in order for us to advance our careers or relationships.

For some people, conflict is nothing to be afraid of. Indeed, a small number of us thrive in that environment. But for others, it can be highly stressful. For those people, criticism is difficult and exhausting and they'll do whatever they can to avoid it.

By understanding your MBTI type (and in time, perhaps other people's too) you will increase your self-awareness and be better equipped to navigate those difficult situations. This is vital for maintaining healthy relationships in all areas of your life.

Below is a brief overview of how each MBTI type tends to deal with conflict:

ISFJ

ISFJs have difficulty with conflict situations, and would often much prefer to just sweep things under the carpet. Whilst their efforts to side-step conflict is understandable, sometimes facing a conflict situation helps to resolve it. ISFJ's tend to need to work on articulating their own feelings in arguments, as they can often forget to do this and get caught up in trying to please others.

ESFJ

ESFJ's tend to have a knee-jerk reaction to want to fix conflict. This is understandable as they tend to be excellent at making others feel better. However, they need to watch their own instinctual reaction of wanting to make the other person feel better and ensure that they are articulating their true opinion, otherwise resentment may build up when they feel unheard.

ISTJ

ISTJs tend to be quite softly spoken individuals. However, they can be prone to conflict if someone does something that they feel is irrational or not in line with their values. ISTJ's need to remember that people are always evolving and what they've done in the past may not be a true indication of how they'll act in the future. They are better at handling disagreements factually rather than emotionally, but must resist trying to always work from a model.

ESTJ

ESTJs often have a "my way or the highway" approach to conflict. It's not that they don't want to listen to others but as highly efficient individuals, they often jump into the role of 'leader', wanting to take control of the situation and make the call. This mentality may work when there are time-critical decisions to be made, but it's not always appropriate, so they must be mindful not to bulldoze over other people's thoughts and feelings.

ESFP

ESFPs often deal with conflict from a very emotional place, but typically bury their true feelings immediately if they become hurt out of a form of self-protection. They sometimes struggle by bringing up these old wounds when someone wants to hash out something entirely different, so it is important that they learn to work calmly on relaying their feelings at the time, as opposed to letting it fester.

ISTP

ISTPs have no problem if an argument is logical and systematic in nature (which makes them great at resolving work conflicts), however they are less skilled at dealing with arguments with emotional bents. They do not tend to trust decisions made based on emotions, but they must learn to listen and honour each person's perspective

ESTP

ESTPs tend to be good at deflecting emotions de-escalating a heated situation, especially in a work environment. However, with more personal relationships they may struggle, as they hate it when people they love are upset and try to avoid it at all costs. They equally do not like to show that they are upset themselves if they think it may upset their partner. ESTP's would benefit from voicing their frustrations and emotions son after they feel them, as well as listening to their partner without instantly trying to fix things. Conflict is not always a commentary on the quality of a relationship.

ISFP

ISFPs are usually quite easy-going and happy to follow the lead of others when working towards a goal, which means they don't tend to engage with much work-related conflict. Outside of work in their personal relationships they absolutely loathe fighting. Because of this, they have a tendency to bury their own hurts, allowing that pain to grow deeper and more profound. They sometimes struggle to express themselves clearly, tending to rely on actions as opposed to words. ISFP's would benefit from learning to hash it out when needed, as it'll be like ripping off a plaster – one quick sting but then they'll be on the path to healing. They should set time aside to get their feelings across clearly to those they love.

ENFP

ENFPs are passionate folk, who have no problem arguing for the rights of others (if it's a cause they believe in). This said, they often don't stand up for themselves enough and have a tendency to completely shut down if someone hits a raw nerve in conflict. ENFP's would benefit from letting other people see their vulnerable side once in a while. They often think others won't fully understand or accept them, but they should give people the chance.

INFP

INFPs are classically conflict-avoidant. They tend to be sensitive and empathetic, always trying to avoid hurting others. This is admirable of course, but they must speak up for themselves when necessary. INFP's would handle conflict better if they have time to consider, gather their thoughts and what they want to say, and then come back once things have cooled down.

ENFJ

ENFJs are known as mediators. They tend to be excellent communicators and good at resolving conflict between other people. However, they may become increasingly emotional during conflict as they try to manage their feelings and the feelings of others involved. They would benefit from not 'hurrying' to resolve the conflict just because its uncomfortable for them, as this can result in it not being fully dealt with. They also have a tendency to be overly self-critical.

INFJ

INFJs don't avoid conflict aggressively, but they do like keeping the peace when they can. For the INFJ it all depends on the specific circumstances and their reasoning behind avoiding or confronting the conflict around them. INFJs can sometimes be difficult for people to understand because of this, as they don't just respond to things the way most would expect them to. They may back down if someone's argument is more emphatic than theirs but should learn to stand their ground and follow their intuition on what's worth speaking up about, as it's usually dead on.

INTJ

INTJs come across as know-it-alls sometimes, but that's just because their only air their opinions when they've taken the time to think through why they hold a given belief. They tend to be fiercely defensive of their point of view, but open to being persuaded if someone provides a more logical perspective. However, when it comes to emotional arguments, they do struggle. They may get defensive with those they love – acting out of hurt rather than listening to their side. INTJ's would benefit from learning to not take a partner articulating their needs as a personal attack, and instead viewing it as a challenge for improvement.

INTP

INTPs tend to stay calm, collected, and analytical in arguments. They will state the facts, and what they mean to you, clearly and poignantly. Their biggest struggle is accepting emotional arguments, since they value logic so highly. They need to remember that some people lead with their heart instead of their head and whilst they may not relate, they must respect that everyone is different.

ENTP

ENTPs are often known as the 'debater type' and are unlikely to shy away from conflict. Indeed, they often enjoy playing devil's advocate just to test ideas, even if its not their own personally held beliefs. This all said, ENTP's find arguments tedious. Over time, ENTPs may start to detach from a relationship if they are having to adapt to their partner/friend's needs all the time, rather than stating what they want. They would benefit from learning to be truer to their own feelings earlier on in relationships.

ENTJ

ENTJ's have a tendency to be convinced they know what's right for a relationship, company, team or project. They usually want to dive in, map out the big picture and forge ahead, and this sadly often results in conflict as they tend to seemingly ignore other's ideas. Since they always think they're right, arguments make them impatient but it is crucial that they listen – everyone has blind spots and not every problem just has one objective best solution.

CHALLENGE 3: FEELING UNFULFILLED/GENERALLY UNHAPPY

This last challenge is a little vague of course, and there are endless specific reasons why an individual may come to feel unfulfilled or generally unhappy. However, each MBTI type has certain triggers which pose more of an issue for them than for others.

By having a clearer understanding about what does and does not make you happy, you'll be better equipped to make changes in the areas of your life where your needs are not being met, or your preferences are falling by the wayside. As a coach you can help support this process and hopefully your client will end up feeling more fulfilled.

Below is a brief overview of some of the themes in life that can leave each type feeling unfulfilled or unhappy:

ENFP

ENFP's are likely to lose their sparkle and become unhappy if they feel like they are stuck doing the same thing day after day. Repetition has a tendency to make them feel listless and apathetic. They crave a life that is full to the brim of potential, opportunities and freedom. They are happy with the future being unknown and living with possibility gives their life meaning. ENFPs may also become unhappy if they are alone too much, have a lack of autonomy or have their ideas ignored or dismissed.

ENTP

ENTP's will become unhappy if life doesn't offer enough variety or spontaneity to them. They crave new ideas, innovation and exploration. They tend to want a lot of personal autonomy in order to pursue their passions and ideas. Other things that may contribute to their unhappiness include not getting enough time with other people, being inside too long and having to conform to a rigid schedule.

INFP

INFP's want to live a life that aligns with their purpose and moral code, so doing a job that lacks meaning or being surrounded by people who don't seem to care about what is important to them will lead to feelings of unhappiness. INFP's struggle when they feel their values are being dismissed, ignored or pushed aside. Equally, they need to feel like there is room for imagination in their lives and hate being stuck in the same routine day after day. Other things that they may struggle with include if they have a lack of meaningful, deep relationships or if they don't get enough time alone.

INTP

INTP's may end up experiencing feelings of unhappiness if they are surrounded by people who only seem to care about surface-level things. They are constantly on the quest for new information. Similarly to the INFP, a lack of close authentic friendships as well as a lack of enough alone time will be a struggle for the INTP. They also tend to detest too much predictability in their lives.

ENFJ

ENFJ's crave deep, honest conversation and companionship. Not having a sense of community and lacking intimate friendships will lead to feelings of unhappiness for most ENFJs. They also tend to feel unfulfilled if they lack meaningful work – they want to see a real human impact in what they do.

ENTJ

ENTJ's often feel unfulfilled if they are stuck doing menial tasks day after day without freedom for progress or innovation. This is why many ENTJ's pursue entrepreneurship or positions where they are given a lot of freedom and personal control. They equally struggle if they feel stuck in relationships or conversations that are focused on the shallow things in life, as they have a deep and philosophical nature and crave thought-provoking and intellectual discussions. Without this life can feel boring and meaningless.

INFJ

A lack of independence and/or sense of purpose in life will lead to feelings of unfulfillment for an INFJ. They tend to spend a lot of time imagining and thinking about the future, so if this is taken away from them then they will struggle. Being micro-managed or stuck in a controlling relationship will lead to feelings of frustration. Equally if relationships seem shallow or one-sided then the INFJ will struggle.

INTJ

INTJ's need a signature vision and some level of clarity about the future to feel okay. Being stuck in the present or past can be a struggle for them. Controlling relationships, a repetitive job or people dismissing their ideas will have them feeling very frustrated. They must ensure they get their alone time in these situations to let their mind wander without restrictions to hopefully have revelations that can alter and improve their current situation.

ESFP

ESFP's crave variety and action, so they will feel unfulfilled if their life becomes controlled or slow-paced. Lacking freedom will have an ESFP feeling 'stuck' – they want to be able to get up, move around, see new places and try new things. They can also feel unhappy if they lack meaningful relationships as they crave intimacy and a sense of connection with people.

ESTP

Similar to the ESFP, ESTP's crave independence and variety in their lives. If they have a restricted or sedentary existence then they are unlikely to feel fulfilled. Being stuck in a stagnant 9-5 job with no room for innovation is likely to make them feel drained. Equally controlling relationships will leave them restless and a lack of outside stimulation will lead to boredom very quickly.

ISFP

ISFP's crave a life of meaning. If they feel that their job or relationship does not align with their values then they are unlikely to be happy. Ideally, their lifestyle needs to be in harmony with what they feel really matters and their own personal code of ethics. Rules, corruption or micro-management are usually things that ISFP's struggle with. They equally like to be able to spend time outdoors and be spontaneous. Financial stress or rigid deadlines will upset them.

ISTP

ISTP's want to feel an overarching sense of purpose in their lives and may feel deflated in its absence. They tend to crave a singular purpose, something that they can master completely. They tend to feel drained if they are not given enough autonomy to experiment, explore and think. A lot of ISTP's struggle to be around a lot of people for prolonged periods, such as big open-plan offices. They need to re-energise by getting some space to themselves on a regular basis.

ESTJ

ESTJ's crave efficiency, order and dependability. If their environment feels messy and haphazard, then they can experience feelings of stress, and if they are unable to do anything about it, then that can turn to feelings of emptiness and sadness. ESTJ's crave a certain amount of control in their life and if relationships or rules don't allow that, then they can struggle. Spending excessive time alone can also be a problem for this type.

ISFJ

ISFJ's highly value continuity and stability. If their world feels unstable, unpredictable, and chaotic they tend to feel anxious and defeated. They also really value close, authentic friendships – they don't need a lot of friends – but at least one close friendship is required to give them peace of mind and comfort during hard times.

ISTJ

ISTJ's love to have a routine and a sense of order in their lives. If, for whatever reason, they don't have this then they can end up feeling lost and listless. They do best in settings where they can have some semblance of control and structure.

ESFJ

Disharmony is particularly stressful for an ESFJ. They crave an environment where everyone is doing their part and valuing one another. If the people that they care about are not feeling happy then an ESFJ is likely to feel like a failure for not being able to help and may end up unhappy themselves. ESFJ's also struggle to be alone for too long.

I hope these three examples have demonstrated how, by understanding your client's MBTI type, the guidance and support you can give a client can be tailored accordingly for optimum impact.

MBTI is a reliable and valid tool that will increase your versatility as a coach and help to deepen the self-awareness and broaden the perspectives of both you and your clients. To get the most out of it, you will need to dedicate some time to learning about the different types and the theory behind them. There are several good books on the market designed to help you do this, so my advice would be to do some research and purchase one.

N is for NLP

You will have noticed that there have already been multiple mentions of NLP in this handbook, but we will now look into this methodology in more depth.

Created by Richard Bandler and John Grinder in back in 1972, NLP stands for Neuro-linguistic programming[20].

Described as a methodology rather than a theory, as well as "an attitude of curiosity that leaves behind a trail of techniques", the name can be broken down as follows:

- **Neuro** – refers to our nervous system. We experience the world through our five senses and that information goes through neurological connections in both our brains and bodies. The results of these create our experience of life
- **Linguistic** – refers to all verbal & non-verbal communication. Human communication is a system through which we try to describe & given meaning

to our experiences. We do this by describing pictures, sounds and feelings
- **Programming** – refers to how we put these two things together to produce a sequence of instructions for ourselves. This creates the patterns that we run & the outcome these patterns produce. These patterns become habits and sometimes last a lifetime.

NLP is a method of influencing brain behaviour (neuro) using language and other types of communication (linguistic) to enable a person to "recode" the way the brain responds to stimuli and manifest new and better behaviours (programming).

In terms of how NLP relates to coaching, NLP can be described as a *type* of coaching (and many people would argue that it's the best type). Regardless of where you stand on that, most people in the field agree that, as a minimum, it is important to have a good understanding of what NLP stands for.

In NLP there are 18 presuppositions (or principles). They are considered to be working hypotheses as opposed to hard truths, and can be split into the following categories:

GENERAL PRINCIPLES:

1. NLP is a model rather than a theory – and it is the study of subjective experience.
2. NLP is a generative rather than a repair model – it emphasises finding solutions rather than analysing

causes – and in NLP we always add choices, rather than take these away.

3. Mind and body are part of the one system
4. All human behaviour has a structure
5. External behaviour is the result of how a person uses their representational systems
6. If one human can do something then, potentially, anyone can.
7. Conscious mind capacity is very limited – supposedly to around 5-9 chunks of information.

INTERACTING WITH OTHERS:

1. Take responsibility for how others respond to you. (The meaning of your communication is the response you get)
2. Act as if people have all the mental and emotional resources they need even if they do not currently recognise this.
3. Discover the other person's perceptions before you begin to influence them. (Meet people in their own unique model of the world)
4. Recognise that in any situation a person is making the best choice with the resources which they currently perceive as being available to them.
5. Recognise that each person's 'truth' is true for them even if it differs from your 'truth' – since any person's

internal view of reality is just that – a 'version' of reality. (The map is not the territory)

6. Recognise that people interact with their internal versions of reality rather than with pure, sensory-based, input.

PERSONAL DEVELOPMENT & STATE MANAGEMENT:

1. Enhance your behavioural and attitudinal flexibility. (In any interaction the person with the greatest behavioural flexibility has most influence on the outcome)
2. Act as if there is a solution to every problem.
3. Recognise the other person's Identity or Self Image – by distinguishing between their behaviour and their identity or self-image.
4. Act as if every behaviour is/was a means of fulfilling a positive intention, at some level, in a person's life.
5. Redefine mistakes as feedback – and change what you are doing if what you are doing is not working.

These 'working principles or presuppositions have been around since the early days of NLP and are a guide on how best to use NLP.

There are hundreds of NLP-inspired techniques that you can use in coaching, and several of the models and techniques we've already covered in this book have their roots firmly within it.

When I was completing my NLP Practitioner qualification, my trainer said *"Coaches that don't use NLP simply have to work so much harder to get their clients results"*

For now, I will run through three quick and simple NLP exercises to give you an idea of how they work.

EXERCISE 1

This exercise is useful if your client is presenting in a 'state' (mood) that is not serving them. Take your client through these four simple steps in order to try and shift your client's perspective:

1. Ask your client to close their eyes & think about what is making them feel bad.

2. Encourage them to think about this thing from a totally different perspective. Try one or several of the following:

    Through the eyes of the other person involved (if there is one)

    From the perspective of calm, excited, accepting (or any other positive emotion that may fit)

    From a bird's eye view

3. Ask them what there is to learn from this new perspective

4. Encourage them to action this brand-new lesson

It sounds very simple, but when we look at situations from different perspectives, we get out of our own head and are more likely to see things for what they really are.

Not only does it calm us down and lessen the effect of the negative emotion, but it also allows the mind to detach itself from the outcome to become more solutions and ideas focused.

Using this exercise when your client is experiencing unwanted negative emotions will allow them to feel much calmer, much more resourceful and a lot more prepared for success.

EXERCISE 2

This second exercise is something you may want to try on your client if they are *repeatedly* experiencing a state or mood that is not serving them. Let's use the example of anxiety around public speaking.

1. Ask the client if they can recall a recent (or particularly powerful) incident in which this occurred.
2. Ask the client to rate how they feel when they recall this experience, which 1 being absolutely fine, and 10 being terrible
3. Ask the client to close their eyes and conjure up an image in their minds eye when they are recalling this memory
4. Ask the client to recall what sounds are playing in this memory, be it background noise or their own inner dialogue at the time

5. Ask the client to identify the physical feeling in their bodies that they experience during this incident, and get them to try and work out which direction the feeling is moving in (e.g. sinking into the stomach or moving upwards into the chest)

6. Once the client has gone through these stages, get them to open their eyes and 'break state'. An easy way to do this is just to ask them to find three things in their current surrounding that are the colour blue, for example.

7. Now ask the client to get that memory back again.

8. Once they are back to that place, ask them to conjure up the image associated with the memory, but this time to slowly drain all of the colour out of the image until it resembles a black and white photograph or short video clip. Now ask them to slowly push the photograph away in their minds eye, so that it is getting smaller and smaller on the horizon, until it eventually disappears.

9. Next, get them to conjure up the associated sounds. Encourage them to envision slowly turning the volume down on any of these sounds, and instead to replace them with an inner voice that is saying "You are okay, you've got this, you're going to be fine" (or similar)

10. Finally, ask the client to re-identify the physical sensation in their body and the direction of that feeling. Ask them to flip it on it's head, and if the feeling is a sinking sensation into the stomach, instead get them

to focus on pushing that feeling upwards away from the stomach.

11. Once they have completed these steps, ask them to open their eyes and give a new score 1-10 of how they feel. Hopefully the number will have significantly reduced.

12. This exercise should only take 5-10 minutes to do, so it is a quick and simple way of taking some of the strength of negative emotion out of a situation for your client.

EXERCISE 3

This final exercise is particularly helpful when helping a client with a critical inner voice. A critical inner voice is something that we all experience, albeit some more than others. It can be defined as a well-integrated pattern of negative thoughts towards one's self, and unfortunately it can hinder our client's progress in coaching.

The below are four handy NLP steps that I learnt from listening to Owen Fitzpatrick (author of 'The Charismatic Edge' and 'Not Enough Hours') that you can use in order to try and combat this:

1. **Change the tone**

    This sounds a little silly at first, but it's been proven to be effective. When we talk to ourselves critically, we tend to use a very negative tone, and with a lot of certainty. E.g. "You are *such* an idiot". Encourage your client to spend some time identifying these thoughts when they pop up, and trying to change the tone of them, taking the negativity out. For example, you could try replaying it in a silly voice (Inside your head of course). By changing the tone, you should stop taking the content of what you're saying to yourself as seriously.

2. **Change the tense**

    This is one that requires a pad and paper (or you can write it on your phone/laptop if easier). Write down your negative internal dialogue and then change it to the past tense. So "I will never be able to succeed because everyone rejects me" becomes "I wasn't previously able to succeed because everyone used to reject me". This shifts the problem from a present problem to a past problem in your mind and therefore changes the way you feel about it by making it less intense.

3. **Put it in the third person**

    Again, write the negative thought down and then change it into the third person. "I am a failure because I didn't get that promotion" becomes "She is a failure because she didn't get that promotion". This disassociates you from the problem and gives you distance between yourself and it, so that when you go back to say that to yourself again, you should automatically make the switch and be less affected by it.

4. **Use 'But' effectively**

   After you write down your negative thought about yourself, start sticking the word 'But' at the end, and following up with something else. The word 'but' tends to cancel what goes before it and focuses on what goes after it, which means that if you can get into the habit of ending on a more positive contradicting statement, you will hopefully focus more on that.

As previously mentioned, what we've covered here is merely scratching the surface. There is a whole series of techniques within NLP that can assist you with your coaching, and I would strongly encourage you to look into them in more depth after reading this. There is a book called the 'Big Book of NLP' which contains over 350 techniques, patterns and strategies that you may want to consider purchasing.

Becoming well-versed in NLP enables you to become a powerful communicator, someone who is skilled at reading non-verbal cues and able to alleviate fears and phobias in yourself and others. It helps you rectify unwanted and unhelpful behaviours and to motivate and empower others too.

Simply put, NLP is about understanding what makes people tick, understanding and using the language of the mind to get better results for our clients. If you are a coach and you are not using NLP in coaching then you are missing a trick.

O is for OSKAR Model

Originating from what is known as the 'Solutions Focused Approach', the OSKAR coaching model is a powerful framework to help your coaching sessions focus on solutions rather than problems[21].

Here is a brief description of the different stages (adapted from 'The Solutions Focus' by Paul Z Jackson and Mark McKergow).

The five stages of OSKAR are:

- Outcome
- Scaling
- Know-How
- Affirm & Action
- Review

Outcome: This refers to what your client wants to achieve, which may be in the short, medium or long term. It may also refer to what they want to achieve from the session itself. Ask questions like: "What do you want to achieve today" or "What do you want to achieve in the long term?" It can also be beneficial to encourage your client to strongly visualize said desired outcome at this point.

Scaling: Once your client has come up with a clear image of their desired outcome then you should try and establish where they are currently in relation to this. A scaling technique is a nice, simple way to help quantify this so ask your client on a scale of 1-10 where they feel they are in relation to this goal.

Know How: Ask your client what skills, knowledge and attributes they have already that will help them achieve this. Questions like "When have you done something like this before?" may be helpful to use at this point.

Affirm & Action: This is about providing positive reinforcement for what your client has told you, reflecting back positive comments about some of their key strengths and attributes that they have revealed. You may want to say something along the lines of: "It's evident from what you've said that you have impressive knowledge in X area". You then want to help your client to determine what small actions they can take that moves them towards their desired outcome

Review: This is the final stage of this model and is used for reviewing progress against the actions set in the previous step, so therefore it will often be used at the beginning of the following session. Make sure to emphasise on reviewing the positives. Ask questions like "What is better?" and "What did you do that made change successful?"

Whilst this model is quite similar to the GROW Model that we looked at earlier in this book, there are some subtle differences to be considered.

1. The OSKAR Model specifically uses a 'solutions focused' approach
2. It focuses on affirming and *small* actions
3. It specifically has the coach and client engaging in looking for 'what's better' - picking up on signs of useful change and amplifying them for the next steps.
4. The whole OSKAR model can be taught as a set of tools rather than a process - not every element needs to be used every time

Give both the GROW and the OSKAR models a try, and see which work best for you in your coaching work.

P is for Progress Reviews

As we have touched upon already, having goals and goal-setting within the coaching process is integral to coaching efficacy. But there is little point in setting a goal with a client if you will never know whether they were successful or not, and therefore reviewing a client's progress is crucial.

You will find that some clients have goals which are tangible, such as getting a promotion or getting healthier, whereas other clients may have vaguer goals like "to be happier" or "have more confidence". Either way, their progress can still be measured as long as the goals that were set follow the 'SMART' rule (specific, measurement, achievable, realistic, timely).

Once a client has verbalised a goal to you, ensure that you have recorded and measured this in some way. For example, if a client has said they want to "feel more confident" then ask them on a scale of 1-10 how confident they feel at the moment and record that number. Equally, if a client says they want to lose weight, ask them how much weight.

You can then look to use a personal goal progress review on a recurring basis (perhaps once a month) as a self-reflection tool to assist your clients in monitoring their progress towards said goals.

This process should be done in a mindful way and without self judgement. It should include questions such as the following:

- *What progress do you feel you've made towards your goal(s)?*
- *What evidence do you have of this progress?*
- *In the case of a less tangible goal (such as becoming more confident), what would you score yourself between 1-10 with 1 being not at all confident and 10 being the most confident you can be? (Make sure to compare this to an earlier score)*
- *What problems have you faced? Have these been resolved?*
- *How do you feel about your progress so far?*
- *What is still to be achieved? What do you need to do to achieve these goals?*

I would encourage you to create a Progress Review template so that you can ensure you are using the same format in each review. It would be beneficial for this template to also include some reference to the 'starting point' (e.g. the score they gave at the beginning when asked how confident they felt) for the purpose of comparison. If your client can see a marked improvement then they are more likely to feel motivated and positive. Even if they cannot see progress, you can use this as an opportunity to discuss what is not working for them and why, and to come up with a different approach.

Q is for Questionnaires

In order for your client to get the most out of the coaching process, it's imperative that you ask them the right questions early on. If you want to do this in a structured way, then you may wish to consider introducing an initial questionnaire that you issue at the beginning of your coaching relationship, following your Initial Call/Discovery Call, but before your first formal session together.

A questionnaire can be tailored to the type of coaching you are offering, but in general it should seek to clarify what your client wants to gain from the coaching process, along with questions that may look to uncover their goals, values, aspirations or fears.

The benefits of an initial questionnaire at this stage are two-fold. Firstly, it's an information-finding exercise for the coach and will enable them to be as well prepared as possible for their first formal session together, and secondly, it starts the reflective process within your client early on. It also gives your client time to think about their answers and perhaps give more comprehensive responses and means that you are accelerating the coaching process by stimulating their thinking before they even start.

One thing to be wary of though is that a client may not be ready to reveal that much on their questionnaire at this stage, so you may end up with a slightly inaccurate picture of them. Some clients will be resistant to opening up until rapport has been built up. However, as long as you only use the questionnaire as a basis and don't just take it at face value, making sure to explore their responses in more depth down the line, then this should not be a problem.

In terms of how many questions to include, I would suggest up to 10 questions so as not to overwhelm the client early on. You can reserve other questions for the coaching session itself.

Here are some example questions that you may wish to include in your questionnaire:

- *What are the 3 biggest changes you want to make in your life over the next 5 years?*
- *What 3 goals do you want to achieve within the next 3 months?*
- *If anything was possible what would you wish for?*
- *What have been your 3 greatest successes to date?*
- *What is the greatest challenge you have had to overcome?*

- *What major changes have you been faced with over the last couple of years?*
- *What is most important to you in your life and why?*
- *Who are most important to you in your life – what do they provide you with?*
- *Is your life one of your choosing? If not who is choosing it for you?*
- *On a scale of 1-10 how happy are you with your life right now? What are the things that make you happy?*
- *On a scale of 1-10 how motivated are you in your work/personal life? What motivates you?*
- *On a scale of 1-10 how stressed do you feel right now – what are your key stressors?*
- *List 5 things that you feel you are 'putting up with' right now?*
- *What would you like your coach to do if you struggle with your goals?*
- *How will you know when you are receiving value from the coaching process?*
- *What would you like from your coach during your sessions: score on a scale of 1-10 where 1 is not at all important and 10 is extremely important.*

These are just examples, so feel free to personalise them to fit with your own coaching approach.

R is for Reframing Techniques

In coaching, you will come to realise that very often it is not the 'problems' that your client faces that are the real issue, but rather, it is how they *see* these perceived problems.

Our perception determines so much in our life - a problem is only ever a problem, depending on what it means to us. A classic example of this is rain. Rain on your wedding day when you'd planned an outdoor ceremony = problem. But rain in an African country after months of drought = a blessing. The subject hasn't changed (the rain), but the context has, which is the frame through which we see our problems and subsequently give it meaning.

Since a lot of the time it is difficult to change the event, we must focus instead on trying to change the context and the meaning. As coaches, we can do this by a simple technique called 'Reframing'[22]. Reframing is considered another NLP tool, and is a way of viewing and experiencing situations, ideas, beliefs, concepts and emotions to find a more positive alternative for you. Simply put, it is seeing the current situation (whatever that may be) from a different perspective, which can be very helpful when it comes to decision making, problem solving and general learning. It's a great tool to use if your client is feeling stuck.

A simple technique is to ask your client to think about the situation that is bothering them at the moment, and then ask them the following general questions to encourage them to look at it a different way:

- *How could you look at this differently?*
- *What is your belief here?*
- *What could you learn from this?*
- *What good things could come out of this?*
- *How could you empathise with the other person(s) involved?*

If we were to further break this down, there are four specific types of reframes that you can use:

1. Context Reframe
2. Meaning Reframe
3. Gratitude Reframe
4. Other People Reframe

Each of these tries to go about reframing the perceived problem from a slightly different angle. You may want to focus on one, or perhaps several, in order to get your client to have a shift in their perspective.

CONTEXT REFRAME

This is about trying to bring your client's attention to why this problem could be a good thing (or at least have some positive angle to it). A context reframe shifts the interpretation and/or the perception of the behavior. This is helpful because almost all behaviours are useful or appropriate in some context – e.g. eating with your hands might not be appropriate at a Michelin starred restaurant, however, it is appropriate at McDonald's.

Questions that you can ask include:

- *In what context could this be appropriate?*
- *In what context could this be useful to you?*
- *In what context could this potentially serve you?*
- *How has this helped you in the past?*

MEANING REFRAME

This is simply about trying to bring to your client's attention what else the problem could mean.

Questions that you can ask include:

- *What else could this behaviour mean?*
- *What would you like it to mean? Is this possible?*
- *How could it be a positive resource for you?*

GRATITUDE REFRAME

This is about bringing your clients attention towards everything that isn't 'wrong' here. It can be effective but be careful in how you deliver it, so as not to make the client feel like you are being dismissive of their perceived problem.

Questions that you can ask include:

- *Why are you grateful that this problem exists?*
- *What are three things that you are most grateful for in your life at the moment?*
- *What stops you being grateful or thankful?*
- *What could be happening which would be a lot worse?*

OTHER PEOPLE REFRAME

This final reframe is aimed at making your client consider how somebody they trust and admire might respond to their problem. Ask your client to think of a specific person who falls into that category (perhaps a wise mentor, a relative, or even themselves in 10 years).

Questions that you can ask include:

- *What advice do you think they'd give you right now?*

Reframing is a useful process for coaches to use in a range of circumstances. All of these techniques, once demonstrated, can be taken away and applied by the client on their own whenever they feel themselves getting stuck with a particular way of looking at a situation. You will be providing them with a method that can serve them for a lifetime.

S is for Setting Goals

We've already covered the importance of helping our clients to set goals, however, this chapter is designed to go into a bit more depth about how best to ensure our clients gain ultimate clarity, as well as an emotional connection, around, and to, their goals.

As coaches, we want our clients to have a deep understanding around the specifics of what they need to do in order to achieve their goals. Most people are familiar with the concept of goals having to be SMART (specific, time measureable, achievable, realistic and timely), but there are alternative models to consider as well.

In this chapter, we will look at what is known as the EXACT model[23], as well as the concept of 'Well Formed Outcomes' (which is another NLP term). Both seek to go a step further than the traditional SMART goal setting process.

EXACT MODEL

The EXACT model fits inside the 'G' of the GROW coaching model that we looked at earlier. Whereas GROW is a chronological process, EXACT is a description of the 'Goal' part of GROW.

It is designed to take your clients through a process which should help them to identify objectives that match up with their own values.

Here is a handy diagram to explain:

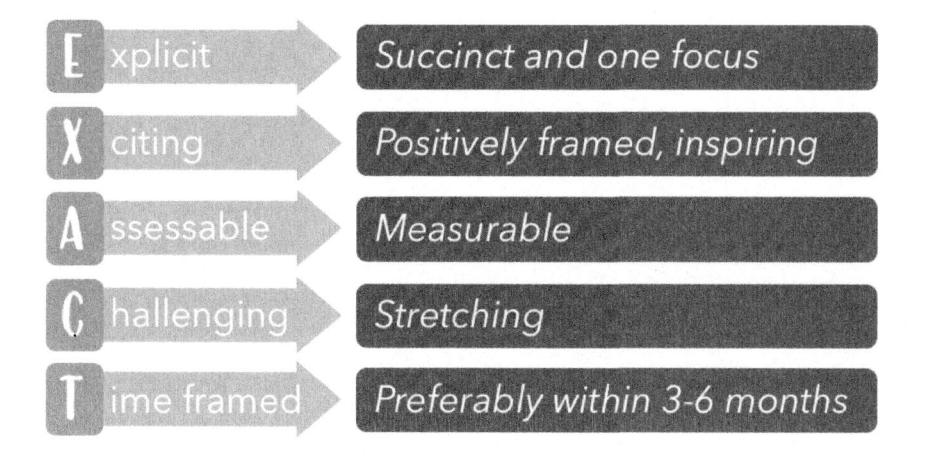

Explicit	*Succinct and one focus*
e**X**citing	*Positively framed, inspiring*
Assessable	*Measurable*
Challenging	*Stretching*
Time framed	*Preferably within 3-6 months*

The reason that it specifies 'preferably within 3-6 months' is because research shows that it takes six weeks to break an old habit and a further six weeks to ingrain a new one, therefore 3-6 months affords enough time to achieve a serious goal without losing motivation.

Following this model when assisting your client in setting goals, can be complemented by structured questioning to ensure what are known as 'well-formed outcomes'.

WELL-FORMED OUTCOMES[24]

This refers to the process of ensuring an outcome has been checked against a series of criteria. If it passes these tests then it can be referred to as 'well formed', which often means that the outcome is more likely to be achieved and is realistic.

In order to reach a well-formed outcome, you need to ensure that your client is following this 7-stage process:

STAGE 1: POSITIVELY STATED

When you are goal-setting with your client, it is important to ensure that it is positively stated.

What that means, is that even if they begin with a negative statement (e.g. "I don't want to work a 9-5 office job anymore) that it is turned into a positive one (e.g. "I *do* want a job that has flexible working hours"). If you can see that your client is going down the path on fixating on the negative, then just bring them back by saying something like: "I understand more now about what you don't want, but what is it that you *do* want?" Focusing on the negative will effectively sap your client's brain of its positive forcefulness, so it's important to avoid this trap.

STAGE 2: SENSORY EVIDENCE

This stage is designed to ensure that our clients have some sort of sensory connection to their goals, as this will help them to be truly drawn to it on an emotional level. As humans, if we can't see/hear/feel it (either in real life or in our imagination) it doesn't seem real, and this means clients will be less likely to take action to try and actually obtain it.

Through asking a few careful questions, we can get our client to the point where they are focusing on what their goal looks, sounds and feels like. This will help increase their belief around the goal and make it more obtainable in their mind.

Ask your client:

- *What will it look like?*
- *What will it sound like?*
- *What will it feel like?*

STAGE 3: CONTEXT

This stage is designed to get your client thinking about the finer details of their goal. The what, where and who, so to speak. Having clarity around the specifics of their goal will help them to make a plan about how to obtain it, as opposed to it feeling like a pipe dream.

What: We need to know what is going on at the time of this goal being achieved. Details are vital when constructing a goal and this is your opportunity to get as detailed as possible

Where: We want to know, in detail, where this goal is taking place. We need to know exactly where they intend to be, when this goal is achieved.

Who: Very often we set goals without considering the other people involved. We want the client to be able to describe the involvement of anyone else that effects this goal. What is their role? How will they help? Will they be happy? Etc.

Ask your client:

- *Where are you?*
- *What is happening?*
- *Who is there with you?*

STAGE 4: TIMEFRAME

Having a timeframe can have a huge effect on our goals, mainly because it keeps us more accountable. Have your client decide on when this goal will begin and when it will end. Having literal dates and times will mean that your client can count down how long they have left to complete it.

Ask your client:

- *What date do you want to achieve this goal by?*
- *When does this goal begin?*
- *How many hours a day are you going to dedicate to this goal?*

STAGE 5: RESOURCES

We looked at 'resources' in the GROW model, and they are important in assuring a well-formed outcome too. Clients will have the best chance of obtaining their goal if we are able to bring to their attention what resources they have available to them.

As previously mentioned, resources can be both internal (confidence, patience, drive, creativity) and external (skillset, qualification, technology, contacts).

Ask your client:

- *What internal resources are required for you to achieve this goal?*
- *What external resources are required for you to achieve this goal?*

STAGE 6: PERSONAL CONNECTION

Sometimes we can be influenced by other people and external factors and this can lead us to set goals for ourselves that we're actually not particularly excited by or committed to. There can be several reasons for doing this – perhaps it's what you feel you should be doing, or maybe it's to increase your status. This stage in the process is designed to confirm that the goal your client is setting is being set for them. Only then will they be able to develop a personal connection to the goal.

Questions can ask include:

- *Is this goal for you, or someone else?*
- *How important is it for you to achieve this goal?*
- *On a scale of 1-10 how strong is your commitment to this outcome?*
- *What needs to happen to get that to a 10?*

STAGE 7: PURPOSE

Most people fail to ask themselves any deep questions when they're setting their goal, which is where your job as a coach comes in. Your client needs to understand the true purpose of their goal in order to increase the likelihood of them achieving it. Goals can be hard things to achieve so your client needs to have a good reason for making the effort. Without having clarity around this reason (or reasons), your client may reach a stage where they just feel "what's the point?" and this can destroy the pursuit of any goal!

By connecting with the purpose behind the goal, a goal becomes much more emotionally driven - and an emotionally driven goal is packed with power and drive.

Ask your client:

- *Why do you want to achieve this goal?*
- *Why is achieving this a must for you?*
- *What will it mean to you?*
- *How does this relate to your highest values?*

After taking your client through these seven stages, they will have hopefully gained clarity over what it is they really want, as well as increasing their belief that it is real and achievable by assessing what it will look like from every sensory standpoint in their mind. They'll also know when they want it done by, what they are going to use (or try to obtain) to make it happen, and most importantly *why* they are doing it.

It is the difference between having a dream, and setting a goal.

T is for Timeline Technique

The 'Timeline Technique'[25] is yet another NLP technique and I first came across it when completing my practitioner qualification.

The NLP Timeline Technique involves using visualisation exercises to help a client revisit past events in their life, or improve their feelings about the future.

There are multiple exercises that you can try, but in this chapter we will just look at one which helps with negative emotions around past experiences.

But before we get into that, let me explain a bit about how it works.

To begin, you need to ask your client to establish a metaphorical line in their minds eye, that represents their past, present and their future, typically when in a relaxed state with their eyes closed.

Establishing how your client views their own timeline in their minds eye, in terms of the direction and positioning, is interesting in itself. The two most common ways of visualising your timeline tend to be what is known as 'in time' or 'through time'. 'In time' refers to those individuals who view their timeline as passing through their body, with their future in front of them and their past behind them. 'Through time' refers to when you see your time line as separate to yourself, usually as a line going from left to right, with the left representing where the past is and the right representing the future. Some people see their timeline as vertical, with the future above them, but this is quite rare.

'In time' and 'Through time' people have different characteristics and attitudes to time in general. Some examples of these include:

'In time' characteristics:

- These individuals tend to get caught up in the current moment
- They spend less time thinking about the future or fixating on the past
- They may be routinely late to appointments
- They prefer not to plan too much and instead 'go with the flow'
- They tend to be associated into events and experiences
- They find it easier to be 'in the here and now'
- They often us phrases like 'put the past behind you', 'you will look back and laugh at this'
- They have their future out in front of them, making it harder to identify the time frames of incremental stages.

'Through time' characteristics:

- They have their time-line straight across in front of them or as a 'V' with either
- straight or curved arms
- They have their past on the left and their future to the right with the present immediately in front of them
- They generally arrive on time or early for appointments
- They find planning and working to deadlines really easy
- They tend to be disassociated from their memories or their experiences

Once your client is familiar with the concept of visualising their timeline, you can follow the below steps:

1. To begin, ask your client to think of the experience they would ideally like to change from their past. They don't need to know all of the details of the experience, just a rough idea of what happened. Ask the client to close their eyes and take a few deep breaths.
2. With their eyes closed, get the client to imagine themselves floating up out of their body, so that they are above their imaginary timeline, looking down on it. Now begin moving in the direction of their past along their timeline. Keep moving back into their past until they feel that they are at the exact time of that particular experience.
3. As they look down on this experience, ask them to start to drain all the negative associations from the experience, which they can do by strongly visualising washing away any anger or pain with some water flowing through the location on the timeline, many people find changing the colour of the experience can also help. Next take the positive lessons learned and intensify them, they can do this by imagining that they are shining a bright glowing light onto or out of them.
4. When the client is finished (make sure they know to take as much time as they need) allow them to drift back to the present. Encourage them to take a moment to notice how they now feel differently about the past experience which had been causing them trouble and then ask them to open their eyes.

5. The new associations that your client has created for this experience will slowly integrate themselves into the client's perspective; this can happen fairly quickly or take a few days to weeks depending on how significant the experience you changed was to them.

The technique works in basically the same way for future experiences too. Here you simply encourage your client to move along in the opposite direction to a future point in their timeline, and visualise themselves being the person they want to be, and achieving their desired outcomes, for example, being more confident in new situations.

You may come across a client who struggles to visualise their future on their timeline. They may just see dimness or dull colours when imagining it. If this happens, you can use NLP techniques to invite them to turn up the brightness during the exercise. This can result in a lighter mood and greater motivation.

Indeed, stacking up a few of these experiences in your future timeline can help to amplify any effect.

It's important to note that at a coaching level, the process does not need to go really deep into past experiences during the timeline activity. It is enough to have the client observe the events, share and then reflect on what the they can do to reframe and overcome these memories. In the hands of a trained person, it would be possible to guide the client to experience and relive the trauma and reframe the experience to relieve the negative impact.

The timeline technique can be a powerful tool both to help create a future vision and to become aware of limiting beliefs that stem from the past. The process requires trust between the two parties, unconditional positive regard, and empathy of the coach with the client.

U is for Understanding Goals

Helping your client to set, and subsequently achieve their goals, is ultimately the most important part of coaching, which is why we give it such focus in this book.

As we covered in the 'Setting Goals' chapter, helping our client to develop a deep emotional connection to their goals is imperative to their success. The reason for this is simply that people are so much more likely to strive to make changes in their life if they really *understand* why it is so important to them. Not just because it sounds good, or others are doing it, but what it's going to do for them. How it's going to change their life, how it's going to make them feel, or how it taps into their highest values (which we'll look at more in the next chapter).

Here is a diagram that demonstrates a simple process designed to help your clients to gain better understanding of their goals[26].

This can be done either in your sessions in a spoken capacity, or in the form of a worksheet for your client to fill out on their own.

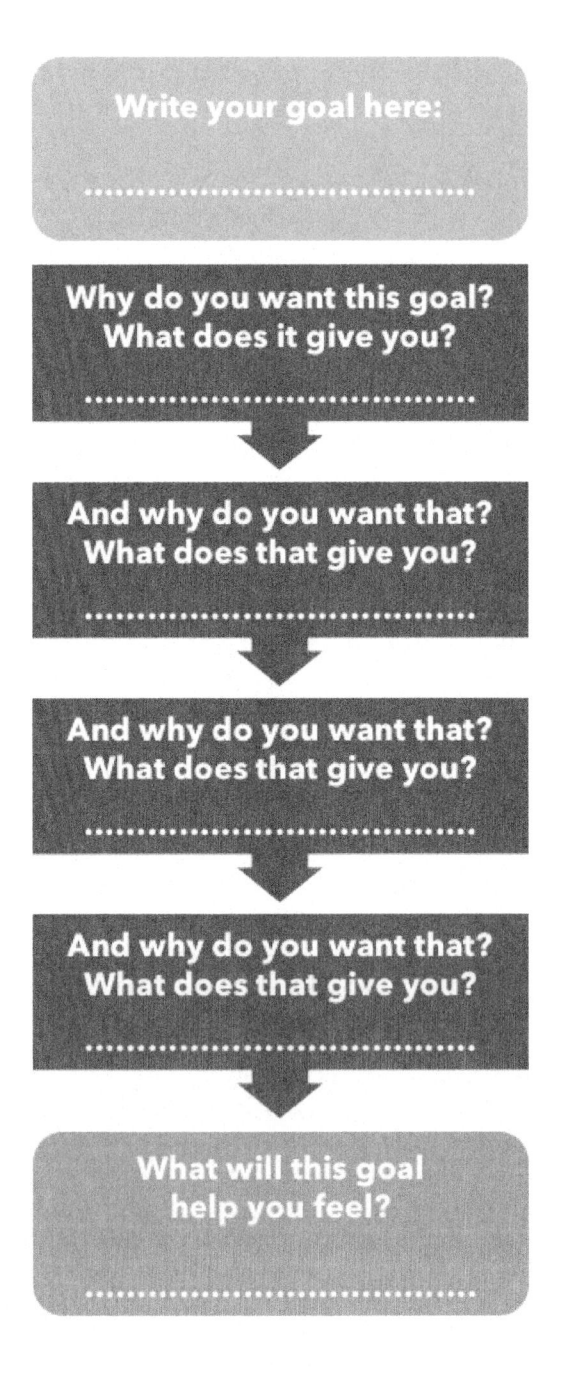

Write your goal here:

....

Why do you want this goal? What does it give you?

....

⬇

And why do you want that? What does that give you?

....

⬇

And why do you want that? What does that give you?

....

⬇

And why do you want that? What does that give you?

....

⬇

What will this goal help you feel?

....

As you can see, the process involves four separate stages of asking your client 'why?'. Each time you do this, the client is forced to go a layer deeper and find the desire behind each answer they give you. It sounds simple but it can get powerful quite quickly.

An increased awareness and understanding means that everything should become more meaningful, desire should increase, and obstacles may feel easier to tackle because your client's desire for change will be stronger than the feeling of discomfort that they might have to go through to get there.

By completing the above, your client should hopefully end up feeling clearer, more focused and more motivated about their goals.

V is for Values

A value can be defined as something that is important to you and something that you will consistently choose to prioritise in your life. There are hundreds of different values out there that one might hold, but examples of a few of them would include:

- Creativity
- Equality
- Respect
- Security
- Nurture
- Adventure

Values are a key anchor point for our identity and can act like a compass to help us to navigate through life. Our values define, to an extent, who we are and how we relate to the world and people around us. When an individual uncovers their personal values, they discover what is truly important to them and can then begin to actively seek out new life opportunities which support them. Similarly, they can then start to avoid or minimize situations which violate them.

It is not surprising then perhaps, that helping your clients to identify their values is a vital part of the coaching journey. Unfortunately, the majority of people struggle to identify their values when asked, so here are four simple exercises that you can use to help:

1) THE BEST TIMES

First, ask your client the following questions:

- *When did you feel the most content?*
- *When did you feel the most fulfilled?*
- *When did you feel proudest?*
- *When were you confident that you were making positive choices?*
- *What was going on in your life during these moments?*

Encourage them to reflect on what the person values associated with these times might be. For example, if they were the happiest when travelling then the values might be 'adventure' and 'spontaneity'. Next, ask them to write down what these values mean to them. For instance, perhaps they equate 'adventure' with trying something new. This will help your client to get to the heart of what drives and inspires them

2) THE WORST TIMES

In contrast to the above, it is also useful to ask your client to consider times when they have got upset, angry or irritated. Often the cause of these negative emotions will be that a value was not being met. For example, if your client brought an example of a time when they were angered by rudeness, then the value they might hold that was violated could be 'respect'.

3) LOOK TO OTHERS

Ask your client to take out a piece of paper and write down the names of the three adults that they admire the most. These might be people they know personally such as family members, or it could be famous people from the past or present that they happen to really like. Next to each name on the list, ask them to write down what they consider to be that person's top three qualities. Is there any overlap? This will highlight more of the values that they deem most desirable in life.

4) FOLLOW THE MONEY

Invite your client to spend some time thinking about what they spend their money on after they have met their monthly expenses. Do they spend what's left on improving their home, travelling, cars, clothing, art, charity, education or something else? Money is a limited resource for most people, which means they tend to use it in ways that match their values.

Ask them to write down the top five things they spend their extra money on, and next to each item on the list write down a personal value that corresponds to it. If they spend money going to yoga perhaps the value is 'fitness', 'inner peace' or 'spirituality'. If they tend to save their money rather than spending it on something they want or enjoy, the values might be 'security' or 'prosperity'.

You may also like to purchase a deck of 'value cards'[27] which can be a great visual aid in face-to-face coaching sessions.

Remember, if your client is feeling stuck or without direction, then helping them to get really clear on their values is the first step in moving them forward. By helping them to uncover their values and take the first steps toward building a life that is in tune with them, you will be assisting them to increase their sense of fulfilment, grow their self-esteem and live a more authentic life.

W is for Wheel of Life

The Wheel of Life is a popular, visual tool invented by the late Paul J. Meyer, who founded the Success Motivation Institute back in 1960[28]. Meyer was a thought leader and coaching industry pioneer.

It is a great tool to use early on in the coaching process with a client, as it can give you a good overview of where your client feels they are at in various areas of their life, which in turn can help you to know where to focus.

The Wheel itself comprises of eight or more categories which are designed to represent different areas in a person's life. You will find an example diagram below, and please note that you can download free printable templates of this from various websites online.

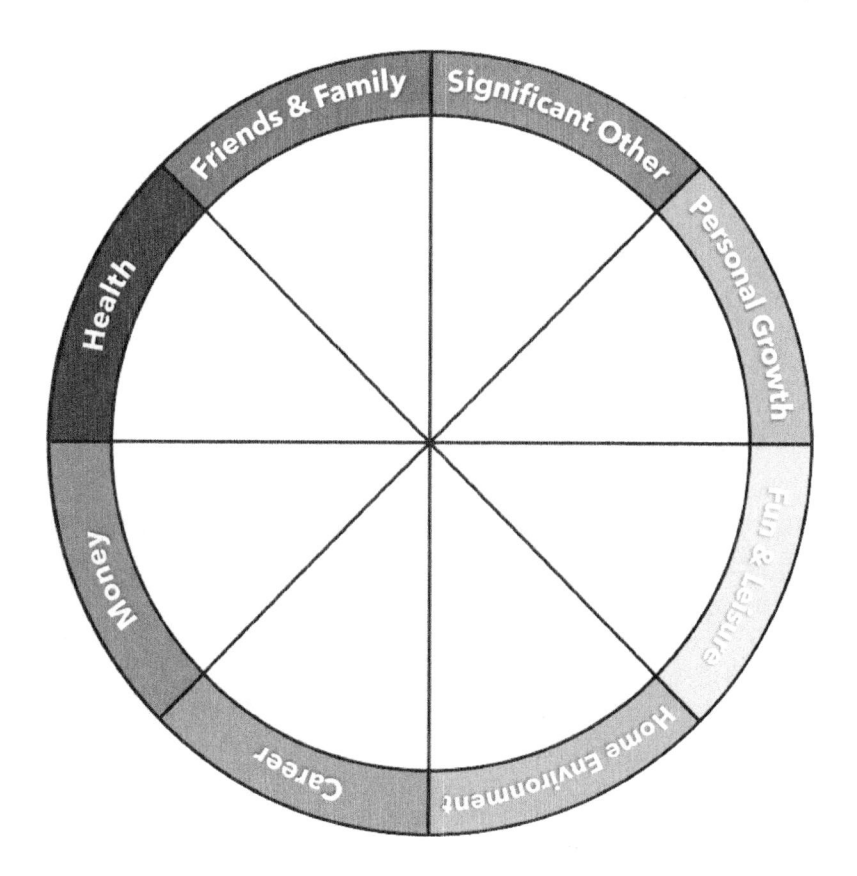

One thing worth mentioning is that sometimes it is worth tweaking the headings slightly, depending on the client and what you know about their life. For example, you may look to change 'career' to 'education' or 'retirement' if the client in question is not working but is studying or retired. Equally if you happen to know they are single, you may look to change 'significant other' to the slightly more generic 'love life' title. This tool will be just as effective with slight alterations.

Follow these steps when using the Wheel of Life:

1. Present this wheel to your client and ask them to go around, giving a score out of 10 (with 0 being deeply

dissatisfied and 10 being completely satisfied) for each area of their life. Make sure not to give your client too long to think about each one, as you want their gut reaction where possible.

2. When they communicate their score for each section, make sure to write that score above the section in question and to also mark their score with a line on the segment (for example, if they give the section a '5' then put a line would be exactly half way in the segment). Once this has been completed for all areas, you will probably end up with something that looks a bit like this:

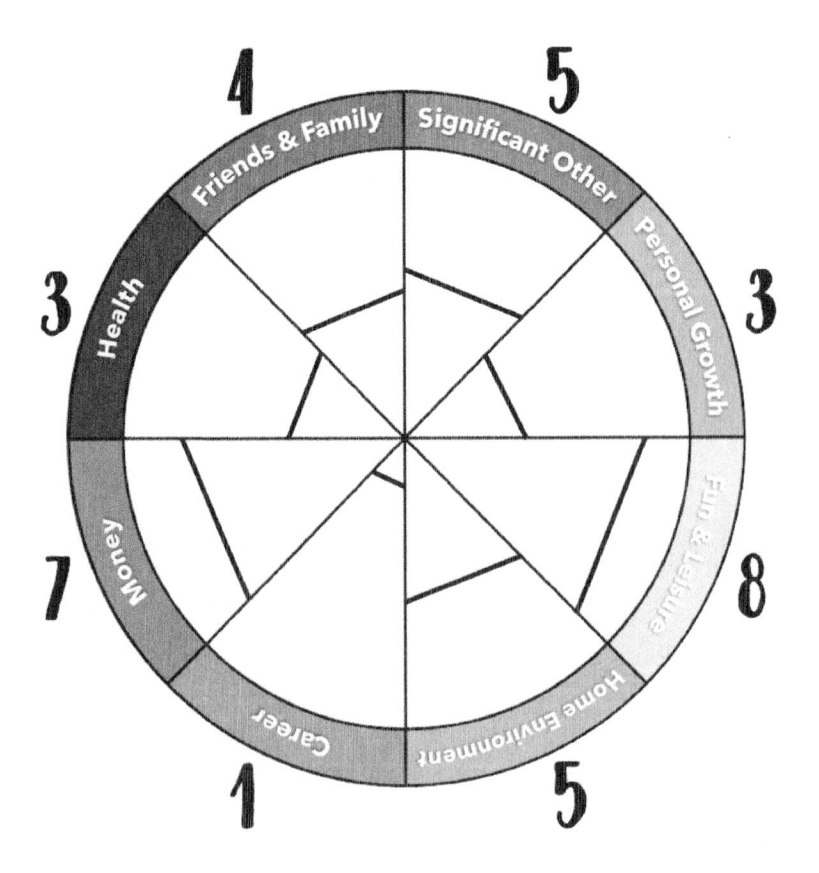

3. Present this to the client so they can see the visual representation of their life and can start to see that there may be a lack of balance. I've heard coaches use the question: *"If this was the wheel of a car, would it be a smooth or bumpy ride?"*

4. Go around the wheel again but this time ask your client instead: "What number would you *like* this section to be at?"

5. As they provide scores, mark those above the original scores like the below:

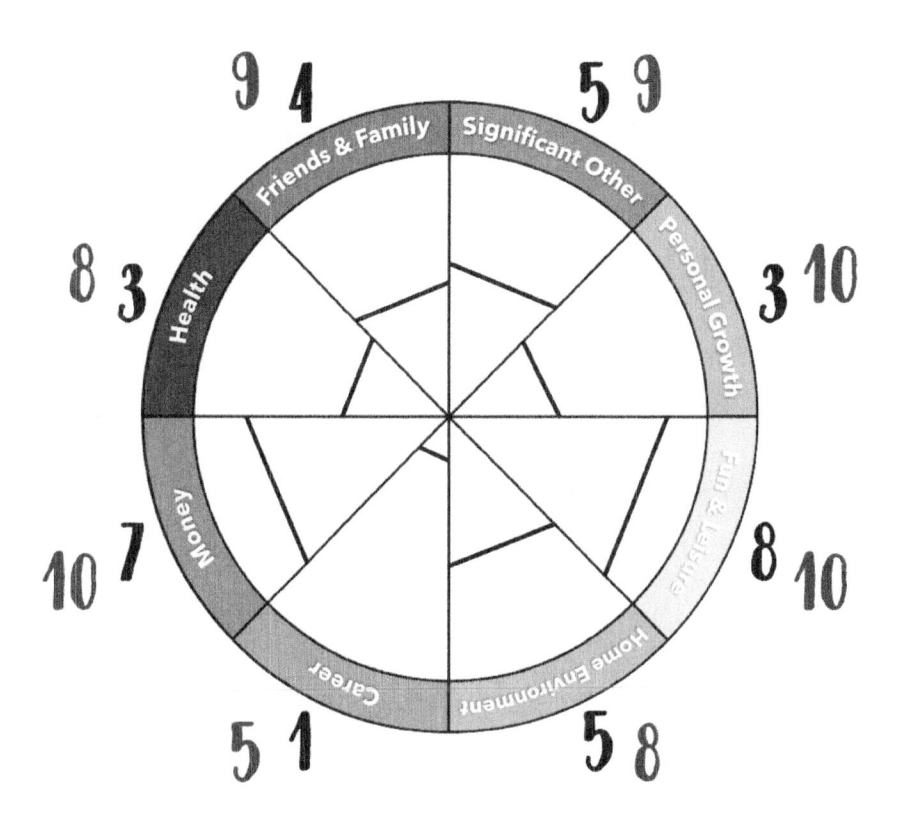

Now you have a complete snapshot of how your client perceives the different areas of their life, along with the ones they feel the most dissatisfied with and the ones that most need improvement and balance.

6. From here, you can start to ask probing questions such as:

"What would you need to do to get your health score from a 3 to an 8?"

I find that this final stage helps your client to identify what needs to happen to raise their score, and this can flow quite nicely into using the GROW model to set a goal.

X is for (e)Xtra Exercises

For this chapter of the book, I thought I would share a few extra simple exercises with you.

Each one is targeted at a different challenge that your client may present with and is designed for your client to complete, either in a face-to-face coaching session or as homework in between sessions. They are all very straightforward and can be adapted to suit the individual.

EXERCISE 1

When to use: If a client is presenting with anxiety

If your client seems to be experiencing bouts of anxiety, it may help them to feel more in control of the situation if they write down their experience and analyse the thought processes behind it. Filling out the below table may help them to spot any patterns or recurring themes, which can be used to form the basis of a coaching discussion when you next meet. The below is just an example of a simple format you may wish to use, but feel free to adapt it as you wish.

Date & Time	Situation	Severity of Anxiety (1-5)	Time anxiety lasted	Thoughts (be as precise as possible)	What I did when I got anxious

EXERCISE 2

When to use: When a client presents with a negative self-image

If you discover that your client has a negative self-image, you may wish to use the below exercise in order to raise their self-awareness around their unhelpful and negative self-talk.

The aim of the exercise is also to get the client into the habit of noticing when they are experiencing negative self-talk and getting them into the habit of counter-balancing those thoughts when they arise.

Ask your client to identify the negative descriptions or statements that they made about themselves during the past week and write them down in the left-hand column. Then, in the right-hand column, have your client write down an alternative statement which balances the first statement by moderating it in a realistic manner. In future scenarios when your client finds themselves experiencing the negative self-talk again, encourage them to try and catch themselves and remind themselves of the realistic balancing statement.

Negative Description of Self	Realistic Balancing Statement
Example: "I always sabotage my life" [Also indicate here the situation in which you applied this description to yourself]	"I overreacted on this occasion. However last week I managed to detach myself and relax more. I will try to do better again next time"

EXERCISE 3

When to use: When a client is presenting with low self-esteem

If you are working with a client who seems to be have rather low self-esteem, then the below can serve as an effective little questionnaire for them to complete, with the aim of giving them a bit of a boost.

1. List 3 positive characteristics that you have
2. List 3 things that you are proud of about yourself
3. List 3 things that you have achieved

4. List 3 ways in which you can treat yourself if you are feeling down, or reward yourself if you have done something well. *(You are not allowed to list anything which involves spending large sums of money, overeating or drinking to excess)*

5. List 3 things you can do to make yourself laugh

6. List 3 things you have done in the past to help someone else

7. List 3 things that you can do to help you feel good about yourself

8. Complete the following sentence: "Looking at the above makes me realise that I

...."

EXERCISE 4

When to use: When a client wants to explore a change in career

Whether you specialise in career coaching or not, often during the coaching process, clients will express uncertainty around their job or career path and may wish to explore other options.

The table on the next page is a simple exercise that you can use in order to kickstart this process.

By encouraging your client to reflect on what it is that they like and dislike about their current, and previous roles, you can increase their awareness around what is important to them and where their values lie. This, in turn, can help them to prioritise when looking for an alternative career.

	Love	Like	Tolerate	Dislike
Current Role				
Previous Role				
Previous Role				
Previous Role				

Of course, there are hundreds of other coaching exercises around these days. I would encourage you to explore more of them when you can, and to keep a folder of the ones that you like the most. I find it helpful to have different folders of exercises for different themes that commonly arise.

Y is for You (as the coach)

This section of the book is the part where we set the tools and techniques to one side, and focus on some of what is important for *you* as the coach.

While you're busy serving others, you might forget to check in on you, but looking after yourself and prioritising your own wellbeing is a vital element of a healthy and successful coaching career.

There are many ways that we can do this as coaches, but I have chosen to focus on three in areas in particular. They are as follows:

- Boundaries
- Connection
- Self-coaching

BOUNDARIES

As coaches, we need to set boundaries in our personal lives and our work to ensure that our needs are met.

A good starting point is to look at what boundaries you are going to set and communicate at the beginning of any coaching relationship. Boundaries are absolutely essential to have and can be physical, mental, and emotional.

I personally believe that the best way to communicate these is as part of your coaching contract. A coaching contract sets out what the client can expect from you as the coach and vice versa. It outlines the boundaries from the get go, which can save you some difficult conversations later down the line.

In terms of what form your contract takes, different coaches have different approaches. Some coaches are content with just having a five-minute conversation at the start where they outline the contents of said contract, and others prefer to have a written document.

Whatever your preference, here are some of the boundaries that you may want to consider including in your coaching contract at the start of your relationship.

- Time
    In this section make sure to cover how long your sessions will be, how often they will take place and for how many weeks. It is also a good opportunity to include what your boundary is going to be with

regards to contact outside of sessions as well as if a client is late for sessions.

- Location

  This simply covers where the sessions will take place. It sounds obvious but you don't want your client thinking that they can turn up at your house for a session if they're in the area!

- Payment

  Include information on how and when you expect payment, and details of any payment plans and options.

- Confidentiality

  Confidentiality in coaching refers to your duty as a coach to not disclose any information shared over the course of the coaching engagement without the express or written permission of the client. Be sure to use your contract as an opportunity to reassure the client that the information they share with you in their sessions will be confidential, as this will help to create trust and encourage openness. However, you must also communicate that the exception to this rule is if they share information where it is clear that they are a danger to themselves or a third party, at which point you will have a legal obligation to disclose that information to the relevant contact.

- Disclaimer
  It can be beneficial to speak about how coaching is not a substitute for therapy. This can help to cover you if, later down the line, it emerges that the client seems to have mental health issues that are beyond your capabilities as a coach.

- Cancellation and refund policy
  Set the terms of when and how to end the coaching relationship as well as under what circumstances, if any, you would offer a refund.

These are three example scenarios of where your boundaries as a coach might be broken and how you could handle the situation.

Scenario 1: A client keeps turning up late for your sessions and keeping you waiting

Solution: Tell your client calmly but firmly that you won't tolerate lateness more than once or twice at most, as you have other commitments after your sessions. Refer back to your contract if you have covered lateness in there. If not, inform them that your policy (for sake of argument) is that after 5 minutes of waiting if they have not arrived, unfortunately they will forfeit their session. If the client is struggling to stick to it, the chances are they are not committed to the coaching process, and by setting this boundary it will help you focus your time and energy on clients who are dedicated and ready to make real changes.

Scenario 2: A client keeps calling and texting you outside of your sessions

Solution: If you have not already done so in your contract, set clear rules for the client. Tell them politely that you'll only be able to take calls and messages during whatever time periods it is that you've decided. Make sure you stick to this and ignore their messages and calls that come through outside of the times that you've set. This may seem harsh but it's a healthy way to create boundaries and ensure that you don't end up drained or exhausted from being constantly available all the time. Don't fall into the trap of thinking that by having a boundary like this that you will disappoint or anger your client – the chances are it will actually help you to gain respect and credibility and improve the working relationship.

Scenario 3: A client isn't paying their fees as per your agreement

Solution: Refer them back to your payment terms and let them know that you will stop all coaching sessions if you don't receive the payment. You can allow some flexibility for late payments if it's a day or two, but avoid extending this much longer than that.

Do not feel guilty for setting and sticking to these boundaries. Coaches that allow problematic client behaviour to continue for fear of losing them with a client or upsetting them will set a precedent that leads to larger problems further down the road. Putting boundaries in place and communicating them in this way is the professional and responsible thing to do. It will help to create a relationship based on mutual respect and trust.

CONNECTION

The majority of coaches are self-employed and this can be isolating and lonely at times. If you work from home then you don't have the social element of a busy office with a bunch of colleagues surrounding you, which can be tough. Coaches need meaningful connections and support that they can count on, just like any other human being.

One positive step that you can take to ensure you feel connected within the field is to become a member of one of the coaching organisations such as International Coaching Federation[29] or Association of Coaching[30]. Both of these bodies put on regular virtual and in-person events. They also have forums where you can ask questions and meet other coaches.

Isolation and coaching don't have to go hand-in-hand. With a little planning, you can find plenty of people for meaningful interactions. You don't have to suffer just because you have decided to work for yourself. Create your own avenues of human connections.

SELF-COACHING

It's easy to feel like we have to be close to 'the finished article' in order to have the authority to coach someone else, but this obviously isn't the case. We all have times when we feel stuck and need a little help, and whilst there is significant benefit to having one's own coach, there is also merit in what is known as 'self-coaching'.

As you will now have so many tools and techniques at your disposal, it is possible to use self-coaching in order to take control of your own thoughts and actions.

Coaching yourself can be a challenge due to biases and assumed constraints. However, by increasing your awareness of your thoughts, you can coach yourself to positive outcomes.

Here are six recommendations that may help you if you attempt to self-coach:

- Silence is Key. Set aside quiet times for yourself to deeply reflect and explore your thoughts.
- Brain Dump. Write down your thoughts. Be honest about how you are truly feeling. Don't hold back. Remember, you are only talking to yourself so be honest!
- Identify Your Goal or Objective.
- Create a Plan of Action.
- Start Small. Identify a few actions you will take and give yourself deadlines. Include what may block you from being successful and how you can overcome it.
- Find an Accountability Partner. Find a person or persons who can support you and speak to them about your goals and plan of action. Ask them to hold you accountable.

By looking after yourself properly you will allow your batteries to recharge so that you can be totally present for your clients and a better coach as a result.

Z is for Generation Z

The good news for us coaches is that the demand for our services just keeps on growing. Some experts have predicted that the coaching industry will grow at a rate of 6.7% through the year 2022[31].

The next generation coming up the ranks, known as Generation Z, will have a large part to play in all of our future careers as coaches. Studies have already shown that Generation Z are particularly open and positive towards coaching interactions, potentially because this demographic have been raised in organised activities where coaches were more prevalent to begin with. In fact, coaching has been found to be the most effective form of leadership for their demographic.

Of course, there are many variables that will influence how to successfully coach Generation Z. Their socialisation, geographic region and socioeconomic status will all play a role and there is no one-size-fits-all approach.

As the coaching industry grows and changes, there are some developing trends that are worth noting. Here are a few of them:

Here are a few of them:

1. **The growth in virtual coaching**

    Technology is revolutionizing the coaching business and if 2020 taught us one thing, it is that coaching can be delivered effectively in a virtual capacity.

    I predict that location-based coaching will continue to lose its importance over the coming years.

    That is not to say that face-to-face coaching does not still have its place – having a live element to your offering can be hugely positive, but leveraging the benefits of technology will be key.

2. **A growing demand for measureable results**

    As the coaching industry continues to grow, the issue of effectiveness and return on investment (ROI) is likely to become more important for coaches. This isn't always straightforward however, and one of the biggest challenges in measuring coaching is that tangible, behavioural change is usually linked to intangible mindsets and beliefs.

This said, I would encourage you, where possible, to keep track of any improvements you feel you are responsible for. Think ROI – how have your services moved the needle within the life of an individual? You can share questionnaires and use various tools to let your clients track and trace their experiences and thoughts on a regular basis to see if there are improvements.

3. **Enhanced focus on positive psychology**

Positive psychology is the scientific study of the strengths and virtues that enable individuals to thrive. It is a rich and growing field, and aligns perfectly with coaching.

I predict that there will be a growing focus on this area in order to help clients overcome their mental roadblocks.

In terms of what that might look like; negative and self-defeating dialogues will be evaluated by the coach and replaced by positive dialogues. The goal will be to create a difference in the client's thinking pattern and life as a whole. NLP techniques may well come into their own here.

4. **Niche coaching will be key**

As the industry has expanded, more and more niche coaching areas have popped up. Nowadays you have mindset coaches, lifestyle coaches, health & nutrition coaches, business coaches, confidence coaches, spirituality coaches, relationship coaches and many more. Not only that, but a lot of coaches decide to specalise further by focusing on a specific type of person within that area, for example men or women, entrepreneurs, single mums, millennials etc.

You may be reading this thinking that having a niche sounds far too limiting and that you'd rather be a generalist, but I would caution you against taking that approach for two main reasons.

Firstly, having a niche enables you to become a specialist in your field. Whatever you decide to focus on will inevitably be something you are interested in and probably have a passion for. This passion will mean you are more inclined to immerse yourself in your chosen field, absorbing the relevant information and strengthening your abilities as a coach. You will never be able to understand everyone. Every group of people is completely unique. Once you become more specific with the type of person you want to reach, you will be able to learn everything about them.

Secondly, only by advertising yourself as a specialist in your chosen field will clients who are looking for that type of help know that you are the person that can help them. If you are simply advertising yourself as "a coach", then anyone who comes across your details will have a difficult job differentiating between you and any other coaching generalist out there. When your prospect knows that you understand them, they also know you can help them. When they think you can help them, here is when they will have the confidence they need to work with you.

The phrase "if you try to please everybody, you end up pleasing nobody" was one that my coaching accreditation tutor taught us when encouraging us to have a niche. Generalists often end up just being average in a lot of areas, as opposed to really good at one particular area.

If you haven't yet chosen a niche, you might want to begin by giving some thought to the type of people you would love to work with, the type of people you think you could offer the most value to and the type of people who you feel have the resources to invest in your coaching services.

Questions to ponder during this brainstorming process include: What age are they? What gender are they? What do these people do for work? What can you help your niche with exactly? Which of the subsections you've heard about resonate with you the strongest? Confidence? Fulfilment? Business? Lifestyle? Mindset?

Remember, there is nothing stopping you changing your niche down the line if you need to.

5. **Social Media Marketing will continue gaining popularity**

   The traditional marketing approach has begun to vanish and social media marketing has grown hugely in recent years.

   On average, we spend 135 minutes a day on social media and as a coach, you will need a social media presence to stay relevant in what is already a saturated market.

   Platforms like Facebook and Instagram provide useful avenues to tell your professional story, attract clients and enhance the profile of your coaching business.

   In 2021 and beyond, I predict that the need for Social Media Marketing will continue to grow and provide an easy effective way for coaches to expand their businesses.

6. **Increasing regulations**

   The coaching industry is currently non-regulated, which means anyone can call himself or herself a coach.

I predict that increasing regulation will likely begin to define various types of coaching. From career coaching to life coaching to executive coaching, required standardised training and credentials will likely become the norm.

7. **Coaching will become less of a luxury**

I am optimistic that there is going to be a shift in which coaching moves from being perceived as a 'luxury' to more of a 'necessity', as people in all spheres begin to wake up to its true value.

I once heard someone liken hiring a coach to hiring a personal trainer (PT). You can go to the gym and exercise on your own and you might see some results. But few would argue that your results will be as good as if you hire a PT. Just in the same way that PT's have grown in popularity in recent years as we've began to value fitness more, coaching is following suit. Having your own personal trainer to hold you accountable and push you forward is a luxury to a certain degree, but a necessity to get optimum results. The same goes for coaching.

I believe that the future of coaching looks extremely bright as more and more people begin to recognise its worth.

Afterword

I hope that you have enjoyed the collection of coaching tools, tips and techniques that this handbook has covered. All of the exercises that I have included are available to download as working templates at www.elliebull.com/coachingworksheets

The use of coaching tools and techniques within coaching practice can offer valuable structure for your coaching conversations. As coaches, we should be committed to keeping up to date with the new models that will undoubtedly emerge over the coming years as well.

Do remember, however, that it is not helpful to be overly prescriptive or rigid with some of these models. To do so is often an indication that the coach is trying to fulfil their own agenda, as opposed to solely attempting to understand the client's issues, and this can damage the sense of connectedness.

Seek instead to remain flexible in your coaching practice and to trust your instincts when it comes to what your client needs most.

I wish you all the best in your future coaching.

Endnotes

1. International Coaching Federation (2003): https://coachfederation.org/
2. John Whitmore, Coaching for Performance: GROWing Human Potential and Purpose: The Principles and Practice of Coaching
3. Association of Coaching, UK: https://www.associationforcoaching.com/
4. Engelmann, J. B., Capra, C. M., Noussair, C., & Berns, G. S. (2009): 'Expert financial advice neurobiologically "Offloads" financial decision-making under risk'. PloS one, 4(3), e4957. https://doi.org/10.1371/journal.pone.0004957
5. Hypnosiswithvic via ProProfs.com (2020): 'What is Your VAK (Visual, Auditory, and Kinaesthetic) Type Quiz': https://www.proprofs.com/quiz-school/story.php?title=vak-quiz-visual-auditory-kinesthetic
6. Honey, P., & Mumford, A., (1986): 'The Learning Styles'
7. Macmillan Dictionary, (2020): https://www.macmillandictionary.com/
8. Covey, S., (1989): 'The Seven Habits of Highly Effective People'
9. Dilts, R., (1990): 'Changing Beliefs with NLP'
10. Practical NLP Podcast (2017): 'Levels of Change: The NLP 'Logical Levels' Model' https://nlppod.com/nlp-logical-levels/
11. Coaching Masters Accreditation Course (2020): https://thecoachingmasters.com/
12. Whitmore, J., (1992): 'Coaching for Performance'

[13] Coach Federation, (2013): JOURNAL Acronym, https://positivepsychology.com/life-coaching-tools/

[14] Centre for Creative Leadership (2020); 'Use Active Listening to Coach Others', https://www.ccl.org/articles/leading-effectively-articles/coaching-others-use-active-listening-skills/

[15] Rogers, C. & Farson, R. (1957): 'Active Listening'

[16] International Coaching Federation (2020): 'Core Competencies', https://coachfederation.org/core-competencies

[17] Skills You Need (2020): 'Clarifying and Clarification', https://www.skillsyouneed.com/ips/clarification.html

[18] The Coaching Masters NLP Practitioner Course (2020): https://thecoachingmasters.com/nlp-practitioner-qualification/

[19] Truity Psychometrics LLC (2020): https://www.truity.com/page/16-personality-types-myers-briggs

[20] Grimley, B. (2015, December 17). What is neurolinguistics programming (nlp)?

[21] Jackson, P. and McKergow, M., (2007): 'The Solutions Focus'

[22] Coaching Masters Accreditation Course (2020): https://thecoachingmasters.com/

[23] Wilson, C., (2017): 'EXACT: A Coaching Approach to Goal Setting', http://www.coachingcultureatwork.com/

[24] Bodenhamer, B. & Hall, L. M., (1999): 'The User's Manual for the Brain'

[25] James, T., (1988): 'Time Line Therapy', https://www.nlpcoaching.com/time-line-therapy/

[26] Ackerman, C. (2020): 'Understanding Our Goals', https://positivepsychology.com/life-coaching-tools/

[27] A nice example deck of value cards: https://hypnotc.com/corevalues/

[28] Meyer, P., (1960s): 'The Wheel of Life', Success Motivation Institute

[29] https://coachfederation.org/

[30] https://www.associationforcoaching.com/

[31] LaRosa, J., (2018): 'U.S. Personal Coaching Industry Tops $1 Billion and Growing', https://blog.marketresearch.com/us-personal-coaching-industry-tops-1-billion-and-growing